# MINUTE RINGS

 MINUTE RINGS

60 Quick & Creative Projects for Jewelers

Marthe Le Van

 LARK
CRAFTS

An Imprint of Sterling Publishing Co., Inc.
New York

WWW.LARKCRAFTS.COM

Art Director
Kathleen Holmes

Designer
Ginger Graziano

Editorial Assistant
Abby Haffelt

Junior Designer
Carol Barnao

Photographer
Stewart O'Shields

Cover Designer
Ginger Graziano

Library of Congress Cataloging-in-Publication Data

Le Van, Marthe.
  30-minute rings : 60 quick & creative projects for jewelers / Marthe Le Van. -- 1st ed.
    p. cm.
  Includes index.
  ISBN 978-1-60059-790-9 (pb-trade pbk. : alk. paper)
  1. Rings. 2. Jewelry making. I. Title. II. Title: Thirty-minute rings.
  TT212.L416 2011
  739.27--dc22

                                2010031896

10 9 8 7 6 5 4 3 2 1

First Edition

Published by Lark Crafts
An Imprint of Sterling Publishing Co., Inc.
387 Park Avenue South, New York, NY 10016

© 2011, Lark Crafts, an Imprint of Sterling Publishing Co., Inc.

Distributed in Canada by Sterling Publishing,
c/o Canadian Manda Group, 165 Dufferin Street
Toronto, Ontario, Canada M6K 3H6

Distributed in the United Kingdom by GMC Distribution Services,
Castle Place, 166 High Street, Lewes, East Sussex, England BN7 1XU

Distributed in Australia by Capricorn Link (Australia) Pty Ltd.,
P.O. Box 704, Windsor, NSW 2756 Australia

If you have questions or comments about this book, please contact:
Lark Crafts
67 Broadway
Asheville, NC 28801
828-253-0467

Manufactured in China

ISBN 13: 978-1-60059-790-9

For information about custom editions, special sales, premium and corporate purchases, please contact
Sterling Special Sales Department at 800-805-5489 or specialsales@sterlingpub.com.

For information about desk and examination copies available to college and university professors, requests
must be submitted to academic@larkbooks.com. Our complete policy can be found at www.larkcrafts.com.

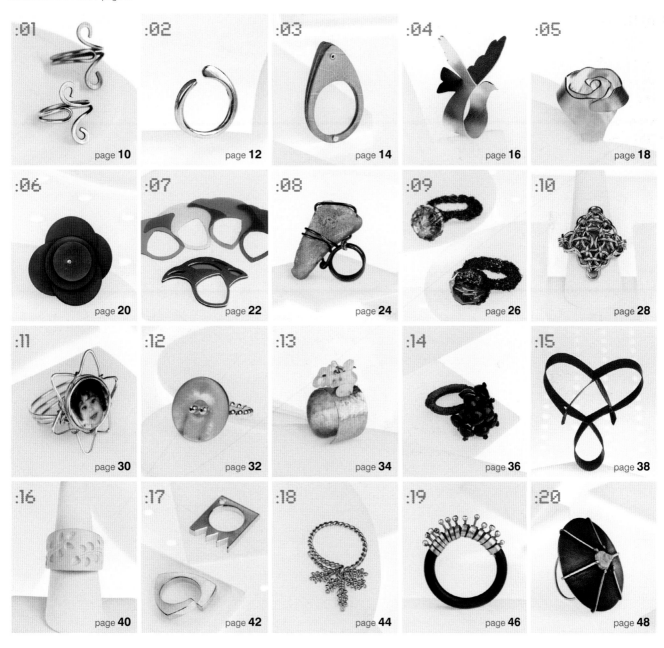

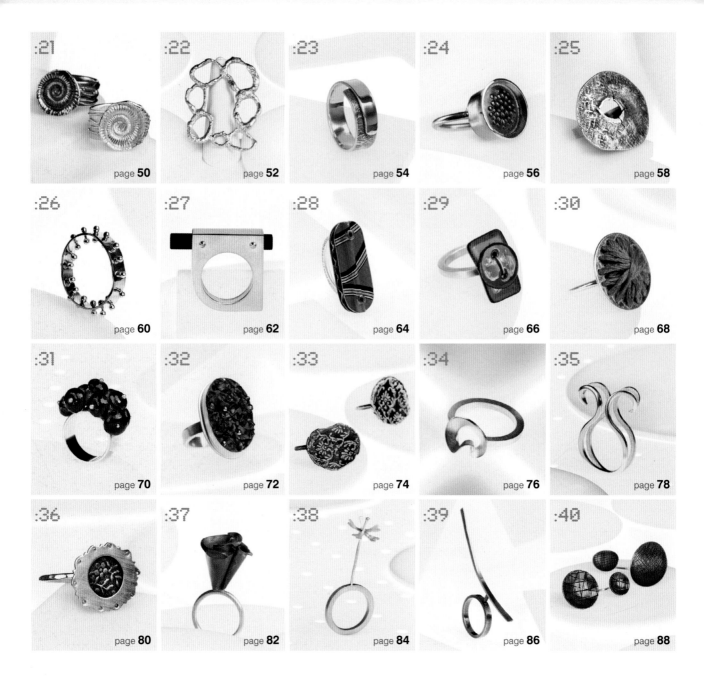

:21   page **50**

:22   page **52**

:23   page **54**

:24   page **56**

:25   page **58**

:26   page **60**

:27   page **62**

:28   page **64**

:29   page **66**

:30   page **68**

:31   page **70**

:32   page **72**

:33   page **74**

:34   page **76**

:35   page **78**

:36   page **80**

:37   page **82**

:38   page **84**

:39   page **86**

:40   page **88**

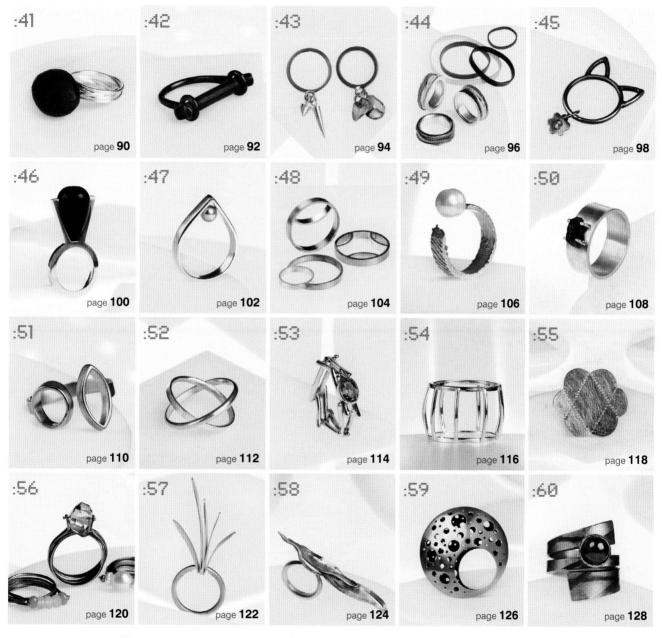

:41 page **90**

:42 page **92**

:43 page **94**

:44 page **96**

:45 page **98**

:46 page **100**

:47 page **102**

:48 page **104**

:49 page **106**

:50 page **108**

:51 page **110**

:52 page **112**

:53 page **114**

:54 page **116**

:55 page **118**

:56 page **120**

:57 page **122**

:58 page **124**

:59 page **126**

:60 page **128**

Introduction

Your hands and fingers are among the most expressive parts of your body. They communicate joy and frustration, anxiety and experience, and love and hope with incredible fluency.

And what's the most effective way of drawing attention to these clever communicators? Having fingers full of rings, of course! From start to finish, you can create all of the stylish rings in this book in just one half-hour. 60 projects by 49 top designers = 12 hands full of rings + 30 hours of jewelry-making joy! It just doesn't get any better than this.

From a distance you would never believe that Karen Rakoski's "ivory" ring (page 40) is made of plastic pipe from the hardware store. Her sizing technique is as simple as sanding down the interior of the pipe. Creating the delicate carved leaf pattern is nearly effortless. Before you know it, you'll have made an elegant and versatile accessory that is a sure conversation piece.

Jennifer Surine's ring (page 102) turns a classic design inside out. Surine gives the sterling silver band a modern makeover by stretching it into a teardrop shape, tucking a pretty pink pearl under its apex, and giving it high polish. The result is innovative but deliciously delicate.

As you flip through page after page of beautiful projects, you may question whether they can truly be made in half an hour. Don't let the gorgeous photography fool you! *30-Minute Rings* offers designs for all skill levels, ranging from wirework and cold connections to soldering and simple stone setting. Most often, you'll only need basic tools, such as a jewelry saw, pliers, files, and a hammer.

The real challenge may very well be deciding which ring you want to make first. Think of this collection like a big menu from one of your favorite restaurants. Everything looks delicious, but what are you in the mood for right now? Just choose a ring and go for it. Your fingers will thank you!

P.S. If you want to add a new process to your repertoire, or if you need a quick refresher on a specific metalworking method, look no further than *The Ultimate Jeweler's Guide* by Joanna Gollberg. This hardworking book covers all the essentials. It is a comprehensive, step-by-step resource for learning metalwork that fits easily on your worktable and is sure to become your go-to source. (And check out the 30-minute prong-set ring designed by Gollberg on page 108).

▶ ▶ Bench Tool Kit

Bench pin

Steel bench block

Jeweler's saw frame

Saw blades

Beeswax

Needle files

Bastard file

Sandpaper, 220 and 400 grit

Emery paper

Chasing hammer

Rawhide or wooden mallet

Forging hammer

Mandrels

Dapping block and punches

Flexible shaft

Wood block

Drill bits

Burrs

Scribe

Stainless steel ruler

Dividers

Calipers

Pliers

Wire cutters

Center punch

Burnisher

Safety glasses

Safety gloves

Hearing protection

Dust mask

▶ ▶ ▶ Soldering Kit

Soldering torch

Striker

Heat resistant soldering surfaces (charcoal blocks, firebricks, or ceramic plates)

Flux

Flux brush or other applicator

Solder (hard, medium, and easy)

Snips

Small embroidery scissors

Solder pick

Tweezers

Cross-locking tweezers with wooden handle

Third hand

Copper tongs

Water for quenching

Pickle

Pickle warming pot

Safety glasses

Fire extinguisher

**WIREWORK • FILING • HAMMERING • SANDING • FINISHING
ADDING A PATINA, OPTIONAL**

→ ▶ Get Set

**Sterling silver wire,
16 gauge, 8 inches
(20.3 cm)**

Bench tool kit, page 9

Liver of sulfur, optional

**FINISHED SIZE
2 x 2 x 2.5 cm**

DESIGNER'S NOTE
The spiral wire ends can be textured with a hammer or other tool.

→ ▶ ▶ Go

1. Determine the proper length of wire for the desired ring size, double that amount, and add 1¾ inches (4.4 cm). Cut the wire to this measurement and straighten it as much as possible. File and round the wire ends.

2. Mark the center of the wire, and bend it in half into a long U-shape, using your fingers or a small dowel. Make sure the wire ends are the same length.

3. Use round-nose pliers to spiral each wire end away from the center, making sure that the spirals are flat. The spirals should be fairly tight.

4. Place the wire on a bench block. Gently flatten the spirals with a chasing hammer, alternating sides to help keep the spirals even. Squeeze the center wires together with your fingers if they spread apart during hammering.

5. Hammer the piece with a rubber mallet on the bench block to straighten and work-harden the wire. Use sandpaper or a green kitchen scrub to buff the entire piece for a final finish.

6. Form the ring around a ring mandrel with a rubber mallet by hammering the U-shaped end of the ring around the mandrel first, then wrapping the ring around the mandrel with your fingers. Slightly spread the spiral ends with your fingers to fit around the U-shaped end.

7. With the rubber mallet, hammer the spirals into place and then hammer all around the ring to further work-harden it and to bring the ring to the correct size.

8. If desired, give the ring a patina with a liver-of-sulfur solution.

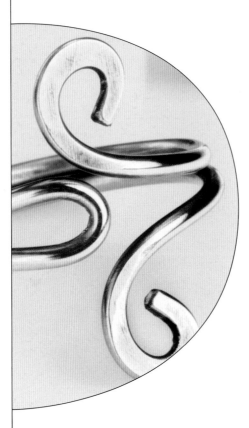

FILING • FORGING • SANDING • POLISHING

→► ► **Get Set**

Sterling silver round wire,
10 gauge, 2½ inches
(6.4 cm)

Bench tool kit, page 9

FINISHED SIZE
2.5 x 2.2 x 0.3 cm

►►► **Go**

1. Cut a 2½-inch (6.4 cm) length of 10-gauge sterling silver round wire. File the wire ends flat.

2. Mark the center of the wire with a permanent marker. (This mark will later indicate the transition point for your forging.)

3. On a steel block, use a planishing hammer to hammer from one end of the wire toward the center mark. Make sure to create a nice smooth taper with the widest part at the wire end. Avoid making deep marks with the hammer that will require excessive filing and sanding later.

4. Hold the forged wire end in your fingers. Forge the opposite end of the wire using the process described in step 3, but at a 90-degree angle to the initial plane.

5. File both ends of the forged wire to form smooth round curves. Anneal the wire, and shape it into a band on a ring mandrel with a rawhide mallet.

6. Sand the ring to a 600-grit finish, then polish to a rouge shine with a buff.

Want to Make Another Ring?

Alter the size of the gap between the forged wire ends or make the ends overlap.

DESIGNER: **JOHN TZELEPIS**

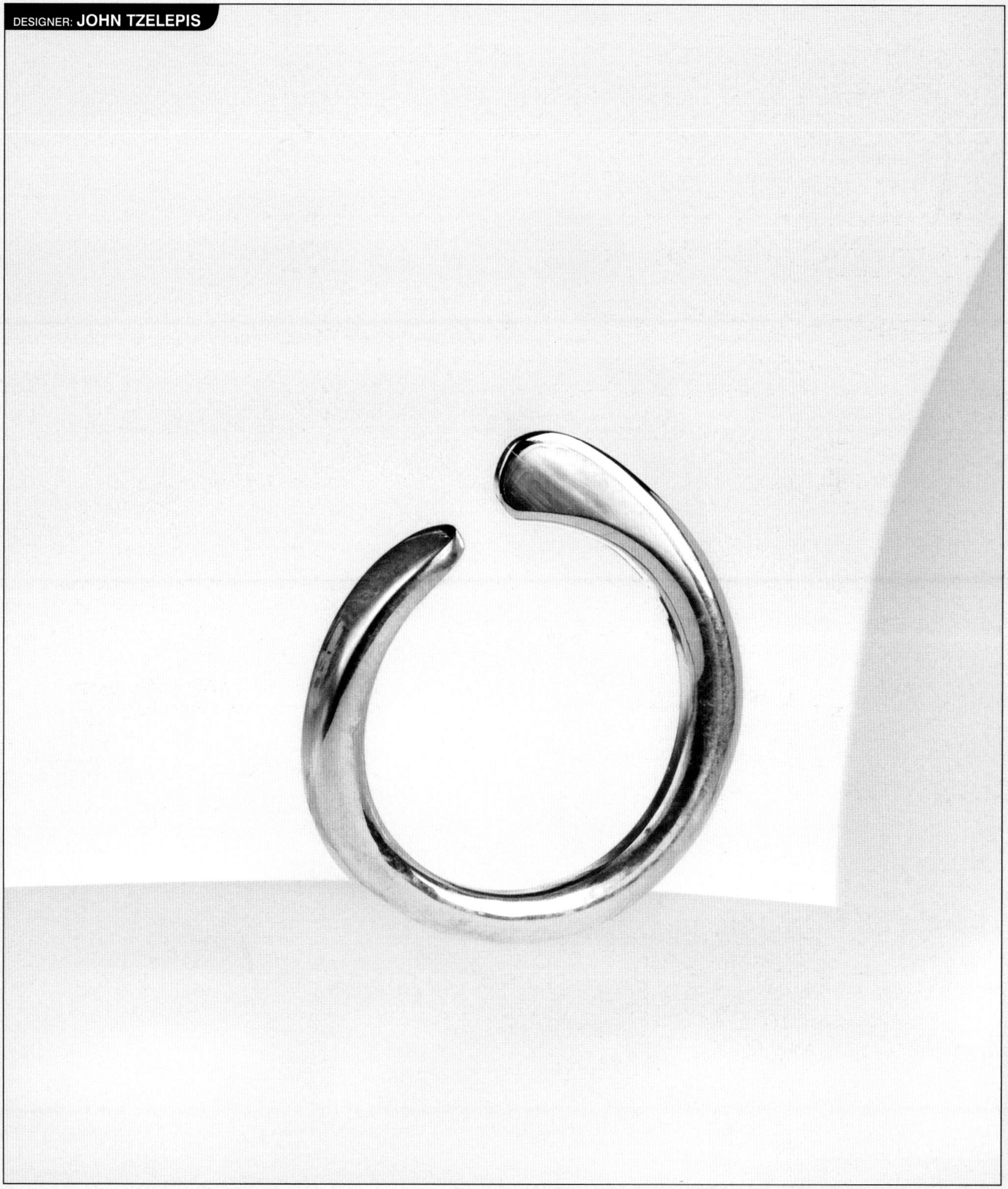

▶▶ Get Set

Brass sheet, 20 gauge,
   4½ x 3 inches
   (11.4 x 7.6 cm)

Organic texture material for
   roller printing

Sterling silver tube,
   1 mm OD, 7 mm

Sterling silver wire,
   18 gauge, 3 mm

2 sterling silver beads,
   each 2 mm

Photocopied design
   template ❶

Bench tool kit, page 9

Disk cutter

Punch, 16 mm in diameter

FINISHED SIZE
3.2 x 2.1 x 0.5 cm

▶▶▶ Go

1. Roller print the organic texture material onto the brass sheet, or use a pre-patterned brass sheet.

2. Using a scribe, transfer the photocopied design template onto the textured brass sheet three times. Saw out the transferred shapes.

3. Using the template as a guide, make a finger hole on each brass shape with the disk cutter and a punch that is 16 mm in diameter. File all cut edges, and sand them to a 600-grit finish.

4. Using the template as a guide, drill a 1-mm hole in the top and bottom of one brass shape. Repeat this step for the other two layers, using the first drilled layer as a guide.

5. Thread the 1-mm silver tube through the top brass layer, a 2-mm bead, the middle brass layer, a 2-mm bead, and the bottom brass layer. Rivet the ends of the tube.

6. Using an 18-gauge silver wire, securely rivet the bottom of the ring.

7. File the ring's finger hole with a half-circle file until the desired fit is achieved.

8. Finish the ring's inner and outer edges with fine sandpaper.

❶
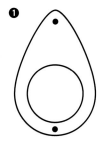

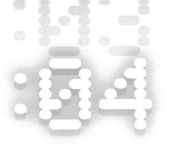

ROLLER PRINTING • SAWING • FILING • SANDING • SOLDERING
FORMING • BURNISHING

▶ Get Set

Sterling silver sheet,
  20 gauge, 5½ x 1½
  inches (14 x 4 cm)

Photocopied design
  template ❶

Bench tool kit, page 9

Soldering kit, page 9

2 pieces of textured
  heavy-stock paper

FINISHED SIZE
2 x 6 cm

DESIGNER'S NOTE
This template creates a
size 8 ring. To increase or
decrease the size, add or
subtract 2 mm for each
size to the center part of
the template, noted with a
doted line.

▶ ▶ ▶ Go

1. Sandwich the silver sheet between
two sheets of textured, heavy-stock paper.
Roll this stack through the rolling mill. The
pressure on the rolling mill should be fairly
tight to give the silver a matte finish and
work-harden the silver.

2. Using the photocopied template as a
guide, saw out the bird design from the
textured silver sheet. Make sure the slots are
exactly the width of the thickness of the silver
sheet. File and sand the edges.

3. Place the center of the metal shape on
the non-tapered section of a ring mandrel.
Slowly bend the ring into a teardrop shape.
Remove the ring from the mandrel.

4. Carefully cross the silver "wings" into
an X-shape with your fingers, and feed the
two slots into each other. Solder the slots
together. Pickle, rinse, and dry the ring.

5. Burnish the edges of the ring, leaving the
rest of the silver surface white from pickling.

Want to Make Another Ring?

File the sheet metal in both directions with
a checkering file. This creates a cross-
hatched surface.

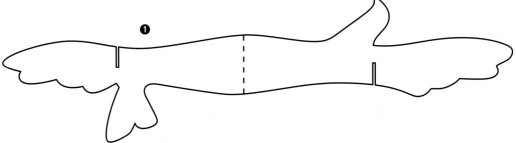

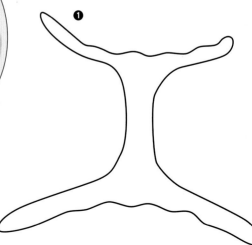

Get Ready

SAWING • FILING • SANDING • FOLDING • PUNCHING

▶ ▶ Get Set

Sterling silver sheet,
19 gauge, 4 x 4 inches
(10 x 10 cm)

Photocopied design
template ❶
enlarged 150%

Bench tool kit, page 9

FINISHED SIZE
3 x 2.8 x 3.2 cm

▶ ▶ ▶ Go

1. Use the photocopied template and a scribe to transfer the design onto the sterling silver sheet. Saw out the transferred shape. Sand the edges of the metal.

2. Starting at the center, bend the silver shape over a ring mandrel until both sides rest at a 120-degree angle.

3. Turn the silver upside down. Use pliers with protected jaws to bend one of the four arms toward the center, forming a curve.

Leave some space between the end of the bent arm and the other side of the ring. Bend the opposite arm in the same manner, forming an S-shape.

4. Gradually close the silver S-shape, and bend both arms with the pliers until you create the center of the rose.

5. To form the external petals, bend the remaining arms toward the center of the rose, using pliers and a mallet.

6. Adjust the spaces between the petals to create a harmonious form. Place the ring shank on a ring mandrel and gently hammer it to ensure that it is round.

7. Rub the outside of the ring with a steel brush.

❶

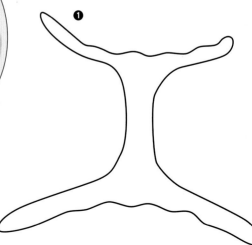

▶ ▶ Get Set

**Titanium sheet, 24 gauge,
6 x 1 inch
(15.2 x 2.5 cm)**

**Sterling silver band,
5 x 1 mm**

**Sterling silver round wire,
18 gauge, 5 mm long**

Bench tool kit, page 9

**FINISHED SIZE
3.1 x 3.2 cm**

DESIGNER'S NOTES

If the titanium is not pre-polished, use sandpaper on the metal so the surface is clean and ready.

Instead of coloring titanium with a torch, you can heat it in a kiln for better control over color shades, or you can keep the titanium's natural gray color, giving the ring a more industrial look.

▶ ▶ ▶ Go

1. Using a disk cutter, punch out five ¾-inch (1.8 cm) circles and one ½-inch (1.3 cm) circle from the titanium sheet.

2. Using a 1-mm bit, drill a hole in the center of the ½-inch (1.3 cm) circle, and 5 mm from the edge of the ¾-inch (1.8 cm) circles. Sand any burrs.

3. Using a torch, pass a medium flame evenly over each titanium circle to color the metal. Color appears in the following order: golden yellow, purple, blue, light blue. Let the pieces cool before touching them with clean hands.

4. Drill a 1-mm hole in the center of the ring band. Use a 1.5-mm round burr to grind metal away from the inside of the hole for creating a flush rivet.

5. Slide the titanium circles in the desired order on the 18-gauge silver wire. Insert the wire into the hole drilled in the ring, and rivet. Take care not to mar the titanium sheets when riveting.

→ ▶ Get Set

Sterling silver sheet,
    18 gauge, 2½ x 2 inches
    (6.5 x 5.1 cm)

Polypropylene sheet,
    24 gauge (0.5 mm),
    1½ x 2 inches
    (3.8 x 5.1 cm)

Photocopied design
    template ❶

Bench tool kit, page 9

Torch

Hole punch

2 pair flat-nose pliers,
    duckbill type

FINISHED SIZE
3.5 x 5.3 cm

▶ ▶ ▶ Go

1. Using the photocopied design template and a scribe, transfer the design on to the sterling silver sheet two times. Pierce and saw out the transferred designs. File and sand the cut metal edges smooth. Polish the surfaces of the silver rings with polishing paper.

2. Transfer the photocopied design template onto the polypropylene. Carefully cut out the exterior line of the ring with sharp scissors.

3. Use a hole punch to make a hole in the internal area of the polypropylene shape. Carefully cut out the rest of the finger hole with scissors.

4. Turn on your torch and set it to as low a setting as possible. Using short quick strokes, gently lick the flame over the edges of the polypropylene ring to make them smooth.

5. To wear the ring, sandwich the polypropylene layer between the metal layers.

Want to Make Another Ring?

Choose a different metal or type of polypropylene to easily change the ring colors.

Add texture to the surface of the metal layers to create interest.

❶

▶▶ Get Set

Beach glass

Annealed steel wire,
16 gauge, 3 to 4 feet
(0.9 to 1.2 m)

Bench tool kit, page 9

White pencil

Sealing wax

Rag

FINISHED SIZE
5.7 x 5.1 x 2.5 cm

▶▶▶ Go

1. Cut 3 to 4 feet (0.9 to 1.2 m) of steel wire with a hefty flush cutter. Hammer and texture the wire if you desire.

2. Bend ⅜ inch (1 cm) of the wire into a right angle. File the end, and bend a plain loop with round-nose pliers.

3. Wrap the steel wire around a ring mandrel at the desired size five times, keeping the coil close together. Finish your wrap at the position of the loop. Make a slight bend in the wire in the direction of the loop, and fit the working end through the loop.

4. Position the beach glass on top of the coiled band. Carefully manipulate the wire around the glass several times. Wrap snugly, but not too tightly, until the glass is secured.

5. Determine the position of the band opposite the first loop and the end of the remaining wire. Mark these points with a white pencil. Add 1 inch (2.5 cm) to the meeting point of the remaining wire and cut. File the end.

6. Manipulate the wire around the band at the first point, matching it to the second.

7. Clean the steel wire with steel wool or a wire brush. Finish the ring with wax and a rag.

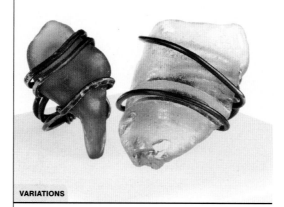

VARIATIONS

→▶ **Get Set**

Spool of copper wire,
30 gauge

Bead of your choice,
¾ inch (1.9 cm)

Small crochet hook

Snips

FINISHED SIZE
5 x 3 x 1.9 cm

▶▶▶ **Go**

1. Use the copper wire and small hook to crochet a tube that is ¼ inch (0.6 cm) in diameter and 3 inches (7 cm) long. (You can use a single, half-double, or double stitch to make the tube. Choose whichever works best for you and yields the proper tube size.)

2. Crochet the ends of the tube together to form a ring shape.

3. Crochet a bowl-shaped setting that is ¾ inch (1.9 cm) in diameter to hold the bead. (Single-stitch crochet will yield a lovely, open bowl.)

4. Make a 1½-inch (3.8 cm) length of doubled copper wire, and thread it through the hole in the bead. Position the wire so an equal amount extends from each bead hole. Wrap the wire tails around the crochet work on the top of the basket to secure the bead in place.

→ ▶ ▶ Get Set

Stainless steel jump rings in the following sizes:

Size A - 4 rings, 18 gauge, each $\frac{9}{32}$ inch (7.1 mm)

Size B - 6 rings, 18 gauge, each $\frac{3}{16}$ inch (4.8 mm)

Size C - 4 rings, 18 gauge, each $\frac{13}{64}$ inch (5.2 mm)

Size D - 12 rings, 20 gauge, each $\frac{1}{8}$ inch (3.2 mm)

Size E - 21 rings, 18 gauge, each $\frac{5}{32}$ inch (4 mm)

Size F - 12 rings, 20 gauge, each $\frac{7}{64}$ inch (2.8 mm)

Size G - 4 rings, 18 gauge, each $\frac{1}{8}$ inch (3.2 mm)

2 pair flat-nose pliers

2 pair chain-nose pliers

FINISHED SIZE
Size 9 ring, 3 cm in height

DESIGNER'S NOTES
To adjust the size, use any 18-gauge ring that is slightly larger or smaller and replace one or more of the size E rings you add in step 14.

To work faster, do not pre-open and pre-close your rings. Instead, open and close "raw" rings as you go. This saves you the time of having to pick up a ring, manipulate it and put it back down, only to pick it up later again.

→ ▶ ▶ Go

1. Add two size B rings onto an open size A ring. Close the size A ring, then close the size B rings. Add another size A ring through the two size B rings, and close. Bring the size A rings together so they are stacked, and separate the size B rings so they are on opposite sides.

2. Weave a new size A ring between the two previous size A rings, and close. This ring surrounds one of the size B rings, but it does not go through it.

3. Repeat step 2 at the beginning of the weave, surrounding the single size B ring with a new size A ring.

4. With an open size C ring, go through the size B ring from the last step. Close the size C ring. Flip the weave over, and repeat on the other side of the weave with a new size C ring. Add two size D rings onto the two size C rings you just added, and close.

5. With an open size E ring, scoop two size F rings and weave the size E ring through the two size D rings from step 4. Close the size E and size F rings. Repeat steps 4 and 5 at the other end of the weave.

Note: Understand where you'll add the next four rings: They will be adjacent to the size B rings from step 1, and each ring will go through the "eyes" indicated. Each ring you add goes through three large rings—a set of doubled rings, and a single "sandwiched" center ring. You might need to open your rings slightly wider than normal in order to fit through, and you might want to thread a wire piece through first, to see the path.

6. Add two size B rings through the first two "eyes," one on each side of the weave. Close the rings.

7. Move to the next four "eyes," and add four size E rings, two on each side of the weave, and close the rings.

8. Add two size B rings through the final two "eyes," and close.

9. With a new size E ring, weave through the first two hanging rings, a size B and a size E ring, on one side of the weave. Close the size E ring you just added. Weave a size E ring through the next two hanging rings on that side of the weave, and close.

10. Add a size E ring to connect the two rings you added in step 9.

11. With two size E rings, double each of the two rings you added in step 9. Add two size D rings onto each set of doubled rings.

12. Weave a size G ring through all four hanging rings from step 9 and close. Double the size G ring with a new size G ring.

13. Repeat steps 7 through 12 on the other side of the weave.

14. To finish the band, take a size E ring, scoop two size F rings, then weave through the two size D rings from step 4. Close all the rings. Continue this pattern until the band is long enough to wrap around your finger. When you add the last ring, do not scoop any additional rings. Instead, connect that ring to the small hanging rings from step 5. Before closing the final ring, make sure there are no twists in the band so it will lie flat on your finger.

↠ ▶ **Get Set**

Dowel, diameter equal to desired ring size

Dowel, ½ inch (1.3 cm)

Gold craft wire, 20 gauge, 20 inches (50.8 cm)

Gold craft wire, 24 gauge, 5 inches (12.7 cm)

Stiff paper or photo

Chain-nose pliers

Snips

DESIGNER'S NOTE
This ring is most easily made in three steps: the picture frame, the star, and then the ring.

↠ ▶ ▶ **Go**

1. Use dowels to make three loops in the 20-gauge gold craft wire: a ½-inch (1.3 cm) loop for the back of the frame; a ¼-inch (6 mm) loop to hold the photo; and a ½-inch (1.3 cm) loop for the front of the frame.

2. Consider the point where the three loops intersect as the top of the ring. Begin making the six star points by bending the wire away from the loops with the chain-nose pliers. Use the base of the jaws of the pliers as a measuring tool for each of the six star points. Space the points evenly around the frame.

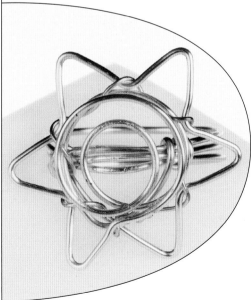

3. Use the 24-gauge craft wire to bind the star "valleys" to the frame. Twist the wire ends together, clip the end short, and tuck the twist under the star.

4. Bring the end of the wire from the last star point down to the center right of the star. Wrap this wire around the ring dowel three times to make the ring band. Bend the wire up and around the three loops tightly. Trim the end of the wire.

5. Use the original wire end to secure the three loops to the other side of the star.

6. Trace and cut out a ½-inch (1.3 cm) circle from any stiff paper or photo. Slide the paper behind the front circle of the wire frame.

Want to Make Another Ring?

Use various colors of craft wire and interchangeable photos.

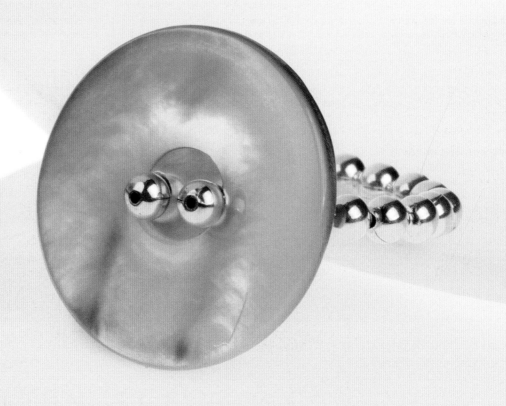

DESIGNER: **ANN L. LUMSDEN**

▶▶ ▶ Get Set

20 sterling silver round beads, each 3 mm

Mother-of-pearl button, 2.2 cm

2 sterling silver memory wire end caps, round, each 3 mm

Steel memory wire

Two-part epoxy

2 pairs of chain-nose pliers

Half-round pliers

Heavy-duty wire cutters

Toothpick

FINISHED SIZE
Top, 2.2 cm in diameter

▶▶ ▶ Go

1. Use the half-round pliers to bend the memory wire into a circle that is 2 cm in diameter. (This measurement makes a size 7 ring. Increase or decrease the diameter of the circle as needed for your desired size.) Leave 3 cm of wire extending beyond the circle.

2. With chain-nose pliers, bend 1 cm of one end of the memory wire perpendicular to the circle. String the silver beads onto the wire so the circle is filled. Bend the other end of the wire parallel to the first end. Cut off any excess wire.

3. Insert one wire end through each hole in the button. Place the end caps on the wire to determine the length of wire needed for the end caps to fit snugly against the button. Cut off any excess wire.

4. Use wire cutters to pinch shallow "notches" along the length of the wire ends. This step provides a good gripping surface for the epoxy.

5. Use a toothpick to apply the two-part epoxy to the end caps on the wires. Let the epoxy dry.

**SAWING · FILING · SANDING · TEXTURING · POLISHING
DRILLING · SHAPING · RIVETING · BEADWORK**

→▶▶ **Get Set**

Brass sheet, 22 gauge,
   2 inches (5.1 cm)

Brass round wire,
   18 gauge, ½ inch
   (1.3 cm)

Brass wire, 22 gauge,
   4 inches (10.2 cm)

7 moonstone bead chips,
   each 5 to 8 mm

Bench tool kit, page 9

2 pair chain-nose pliers

FINISHED SIZE
1.3 x 2 x 3 cm

▶▶▶ **Go**

1. Saw a ½ x 2¼-inch (1.3 x 5.7 cm) band from the brass sheet. Round the corners of the band, and file its edges smooth.

2. Using a flexible shaft, scratch both sides of the brass band with a stone point. Rub both sides of the metal with a green scrub pad to soften the marks made by the stone point.

3. Add texture to the brass band by hammering it with the ball side of a chasing hammer. Polish the band with the flexible shaft or a polishing cloth.

4. Find and mark the center of the brass band. Drill a hole at the marked point with a 1-mm bit. Remove any burrs with a round file, taking care not to enlarge the hole.

5. Hammer the band into a curved shape on a ring mandrel with a rawhide mallet, making sure to leave space between the ends. This is the ring.

6. File one end of the 18-gauge brass wire to remove any burrs so it will fit properly into the hole drilled in the ring. This wire is the rivet wire, and it should fit snugly in the hole.

7. Hold the rivet wire with chain-nose pliers, with the filed end resting on a wood block. Leave ¼ inch (6 mm) of the wire sticking out of the jaws. Using the flat side of the chasing hammer, hammer the end to flatten and form a rivet.

8. Thread the rivet wire into the hole, with the riveted wire end on the inside of the ring. Use pliers to straighten the wire.

9. Hold the straight rivet wire with chain-nose pliers right next to the hole on the outside of the ring. Make sure the rivet head is flush inside the ring. Using another pair of chain-nose pliers, bend the wire 90 degrees right above the jaws. Keep holding the wire tightly in the chain-nose pliers, and use round-nose pliers to form a loop.

10. Make seven 1-inch (2.5 cm) headpins with the 22-gauge brass wire, hammering the ends of the wire flat. Thread a moonstone bead chip onto each length of wire. Loop the wire near the bead and thread five beaded headpins on the ring. Wrap each wire around its base to secure the headpin in place. Thread and secure two beaded headpins to the straight wire length beneath the loop on the ring.

DESIGNER: **CYNTHIA B. WULLER**

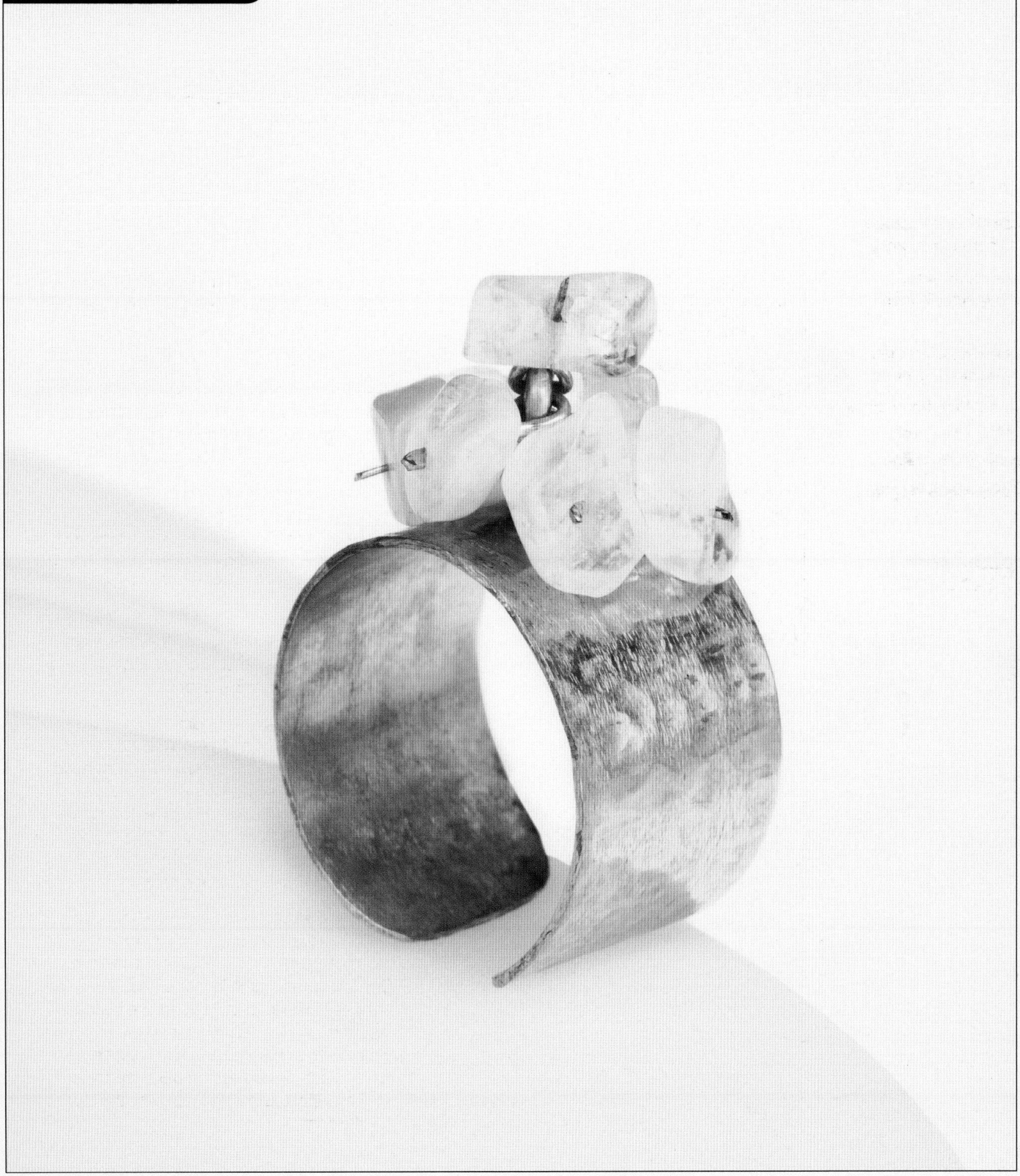

⇥ ▶ Get Set

Waxed nylon thread

Drilled seeds or beads

Ring mandrel

Lighter

**Needle, large eye to
accommodate thread**

FINISHED SIZE
2.5 x 3.2 x 1.9 cm

▶ ▶ ▶ Go

1. Cut five 12-inch (30.5 cm) lengths of waxed nylon thread. Cut one 48-inch (121.9 cm) length of waxed nylon thread.

2. Hold the 12-inch (30.5 cm) threads in a group and wrap them twice around a ring mandrel, at a point three sizes larger than needed (this is not exact, but the ring can be stretched as you go).

3. Tie the long thread tightly around the five-thread bunch, leaving 2 inches (5.1 cm) of string on one side of the knot. (The seeds or beads will be strung on these remaining tails.) Thread the long end of the long thread through the eye of a sewing needle.

4. Loop the needle completely around the five-thread bunch and tie a simple knot. (A buttonhole knot works well here.) Repeat this step until the entire band is knotted.

5. Thread one bead or seed on a thread tail, and secure with a tight knot. Repeat with each of the remaining thread tails. Cut each thread tail to $\frac{1}{16}$ inch (1.6 mm).

6. Seal the knots by burning each thread end with a lighter. Quickly flatten the still-hot ball with a cold piece of steel, such as the end of the flat-nose pliers.

▶ ▶ **Get Set**

Red hard-wearing
semitransparent
polypropylene,
10¼ x ⅝ inch
(26 x 1.5 cm)

Photocopied design
template ❶
enlarged 200%

Craft knife

Leather punch

Leather corner punch

FINISHED SIZE
6 x 5 x 1.6 cm

DESIGNER'S NOTE
You can replace the semi-
transparent polypropylene
with any other plastic or
paper material that is easy
to cut, flexible, and
sufficiently stiff.

▶ ▶ ▶ **Go**

1. Transfer the cutting and punching marks
from the photocopied design template to the
polypropylene strip.

2. Punch out each dot marked on the
polypropylene strip with the leather punch.

3. Use a craft knife and a ruler to cut each
slit marked on the polypropylene strip.

4. Use the corner punch to round the four
corners of the polypropylene strip.

5. Starting from the center, bend the
polypropylene strip. Fit cuts D and E
together, then join subsequent cuts to create
the heart shape—A and F; B and G; and
H and C.

Want To Make Another Ring?

Change the spaces between the cuts to alter
the size of the heart.

Have Time To Spare?

Decorate the ring using the leather punch.

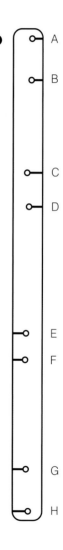

❶

A
B
C
D
E
F
G
H

▸▸ Get Set

White plastic plumbing pipe, ¾ inch (1.9 cm) in diameter, ¾ inch (1.9 cm) long

Photocopied design template ❶

Bench tool kit, page 9

Cone burr, 0.6 x 1.9 cm

Inverted cone burr, 3 mm

Ball burr, 3 mm

Soft toothbrush

T pin

FINISHED SIZE
Front, 1.9 cm; back, 0.6 cm

DESIGNER'S NOTE
To make a different size ring, start with a different size pipe or sand out the pipe's interior.

▸▸▸ Go

1. Lightly sand any manufacturer's printing off of the plumbing pipe. Measure and mark one line that is ¼ inch (0.6 cm) inside the edge of the pipe. Measure and mark a second line that is ¾ inch (1.9 cm) from the edge of the pipe.

2. Mark a dot on the ¼-inch (0.6 cm) line and position the pipe so the dot is on the left. Using a slanted line, connect the marked dot to the ¾-inch (1.9 cm) line at the far right side of the pipe. Saw the pipe along this line.

3. Using the large cone burr attachment in a flexible shaft, bevel all the inside edges of the pipe. Hand sand the ground areas with sandpaper until the transitions are smooth.

4. Use the photocopied template to trace the design pattern onto the ring. The center of the tips of the center leaves should line up with the front centerline of the ring.

5. Using the inverted cone burr attachment in the flexible shaft, carve a groove on both sides of each branch. (A groove cut in one firm line looks best.) Make a lighter second cut with the same burr along each branch, on the far side of the line, leaving the stem with a triangular profile.

6. Switch to the small round burr attachment on the flexible shaft. Place the burr along the stem at the marked leaf locations, and slowly remove the plastic material. The rounded leaf shape will be formed by the rotation of the bit; no hand movement is necessary.

7. Sand off any raised curls of plastic, making sure to round the stems. Use the T pin to scribe a line down the center of each leaf.

8. Brush the ring with a soft toothbrush to clean out any fine grit or curls of plastic.

❶

SAWING • FILING • DRILLING • SOLDERING • BENDING

⇢►► **Get Set**

Sterling silver sheet,
    12 gauge, 2 x 2 inches
    (5.1 x 5.1 cm)

Bench tool kit, page 9

Soldering kit, page 9

Photocopied design
    template ❶

FINISHED SIZE
2.4 x 2.1 x 0.3 cm

⇢►►► **Go**

1. Use the template to saw the triangle shape from the 12-gauge sterling silver sheet. Pierce and saw out the center circle. Saw a second triangle slightly larger than the first from the remaining silver sheet.

2. File the inside of the sawn circle with a half round file. Sand each side of both triangles with 220-grit sandpaper.

3. Place the silver triangle with the hole on top of the solid triangle and rest both on the solder block. Flux and solder the two pieces together using plenty of medium solder. (Insufficient solder will yield pores between the sheets later, and excess solder is easy to remove.) Pickle, rinse, and dry the metal form.

❶

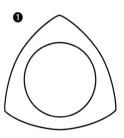

4. Trim off all excess material from the outer edge of the metal form. Pierce and saw out the circle from the solid triangle. File all edges flush with a flat file. Sand with 320-grit sandpaper, and apply the final texture.

5. Find the center of one side of the triangle using dividers. Draw a line from the center of one side to the point of the opposite side. Saw open the side along this line.

6. Protect the jaws of the vise with masking tape. Place one side of the cut metal in the jaws and tighten the vise. Hold the other side of the cut with parallel pliers, and slightly bend and twist the ring, opening the cut. File and sand the open areas.

7. Polish the inside and sides of the ring with a buff on a polishing lathe. Burnish the edges of the ring.

Want To Make Another Ring?

Customize the template with your own design to create corrugated ends, drilled holes, or rounded edges.

▶▶ ▶ Get Set

Sterling silver round wire, 18 gauge, 9 inches (22.9 cm)

Sterling silver round wire, 24 gauge, 7½ inches (19 cm)

Sterling silver round beads, each 2 mm

Bench tool kit, page 9

Soldering kit, page 9

Modified vise grips

Nail, 3 mm in diameter

**FINISHED SIZE
3.2 x 2.1 x 0.2 cm**

DESIGNER'S NOTE
File off the ridges on each jaw of the vise grips so the metal will not be marred when held.

▶▶ ▶ Go

1. Use snips to cut a 9-inch (22.9 cm) length of 18-gauge sterling silver round wire.

2. Place the nail in the vise, leaving at least 1 inch (2.5 cm) of the nail extending past the jaws.

3. Bend the middle of the 18-gauge wire around the nail. Hold the wire ends tightly in the vise grips. Turn the vise grips until the length of the silver wire is completely twisted. Remove the twisted wire from the nail. Use flat-nose pliers to bend the loop perpendicular to the wire.

4. Use a torch to ball the end of the twisted wire. Polish the wire.

5. Use your fingers and round-nose pliers to bend the twisted wire into a ring that is smaller than the size you desire. Place the ring on a ring mandrel, and hammer it lightly with a rawhide or plastic mallet to enlarge it to the correct size.

6. Cut the 24-gauge wire into five pieces, each 1½ inches (3.8 cm) long. Use a torch to ball one end of each wire.

7. Slide three or four silver beads on a balled wire. Use round-nose pliers to make a loop 4 mm from the beads. Attach the loop with the beads to the loop on the ring. Wrap the wire tail around the 4-mm length until it touches the last bead. Snip off the remaining tail. Repeat this step for the remaining balled wires.

CUTTING • SANDING • STAMPING • BALLING WIRE • DRILLING ADDING A PATINA, OPTIONAL

→ ▶ Get Set

Sterling silver round wire, 20 gauge, 3½ inches (8.9 cm)

Brass sheet, 26 gauge, 2 mm wide, 5 inches (12.7 cm)

Buna cord, 0.4 cm in diameter, 2½ inches (6.4 cm)

Bench tool kit, page 9

Soldering kit, page 9

Craft knife

Stamping tool

Liver of sulfur

FINISHED SIZE
2.9 x 2.9 x 0.4 cm

DESIGNER'S NOTE
Instead of stamping, you can buy a patterned sheet or use a hammer or a rolling mill to create a texture.

▶ ▶ ▶ Go

1. Use a craft knife to cut the buna cord to the appropriate length for your ring size.

2. Use snips to cut the brass sheet twice the length of the buna cord. Slightly taper each end of the strip with a flat file.

3. Texture the brass strip with a hammer and a stamping tool. Smooth the edges and round the ends of the strip with sandpaper.

4. Using chain-nose pliers, coil the metal strip so it is slightly larger in diameter than the buna cord.

5. Push one end of the rubber cord into the coiled brass strip until the cord fills one half of the coil. Repeat for the other end of the cord and coil. Use your fingers to gently bend the brass coil into an even arc.

6. Count the number of coils, and cut a ½-inch (1.3 cm) length of 20-gauge silver wire for each coil. Ball the ends of each wire. Trim each piece of balled wire to ¼ inch (0.6 cm).

7. Mark a line along the top centerline of the coil with a pencil. Use the craft knife to make a small divot in the middle of each coil on the marked line.

8. Use a 1-mm bit to drill through the top of each coil, halfway into the buna cord. Use a 1.1-mm bit to enlarge the holes you just drilled in the coil. Do not drill into the buna cord.

9. Using chain-nose pliers, push a balled wire into each hole in the coil. Push the wire all the way into the buna cord. Polish or patina the metal as desired.

Want to Make Another Ring?

Use different metals or add pearls or beads to the tops of the wires to add color.

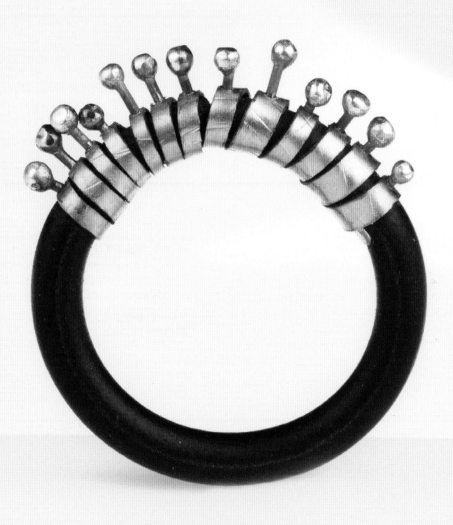

SAWING • DRILLING • SOLDERING • FILING • SANDING POLISHING • ADDING A PATINA

▶▶ **Get Set**

Sterling silver sheet, 22 gauge, 1¾ x 3½ inches (4.4 x 8.9 cm)

Sterling silver round wire, 18 gauge, 3¾ inches (9.5 cm)

Sterling silver round wire, 16 gauge, 2 inches (5.1 cm)

Photocopied design template ❶

Shell, with pointed top

Bench tool kit, page 9

Soldering kit, page 9

Liver of sulfur

FINISHED SIZE
4 x 4 x 1 cm

▶▶▶ **Go**

1. Use calipers to scribe a circle on the silver sheet, 1⅝ inch (4 cm) in diameter. In the center of this circle, scribe a second circle that is ⅜ inch (1 cm) in diameter. Saw out the outer circle. Pierce and saw out the inner circle. Using the template as a guide, saw the circle open. You now have a split washer shape.

2. Scribe and saw out a second circle from the silver sheet with a diameter of 1⅜ inches (3.5 cm). File and sand the edges of this silver circle and the split washer shape.

3. Draw six equidistant lines from the perimeter of the split washer to its interior hole. Deepen the lines with a triangular file, then switch to a square file to make a shallow groove.

4. Bend the ends of the split washer together into a cone shape. Solder this joint, then file and sand it.

5. Cut six pieces of 18-gauge wire, each 1¼ inches (3.2 cm) long. Ball the end of each wire with a torch.

6. Determine the length of wire needed to make the desired ring size. Cut the 16-gauge silver wire to this measurement. Bend the wire into a circle so the ends touch, and solder the joint. File and sand the soldered joint.

7. Use a rawhide mallet and a ring mandrel to hammer the wire circle into a round ring. Position the ring perpendicular to the center of the 1⅜-inch (3.5 cm) silver circle cut in step 2. Solder to ring to the silver circle.

8. Place each of the six wires in a groove on the cone-shaped silver piece, with the balled ends just hanging over the interior circle. Carefully solder the wires in place so no solder flows on the sheet metal. The non-balled wire ends should protrude 15 mm from the edge of the cone.

9. Find a shell that fits in the hole of the cone shape. The pointed end of the shell should protrude from the interior hole, but the shell should not fall through the hole.

10. With the ring facing down, position the silver circle in the bottom of the cone shape. Using your fingers, bend each 15-mm length of wire over the back of the silver circle, locking it in place. Blacken the ring with a liver-of-sulfur solution to finish.

❶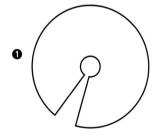

▶▶ Get Set

Art Clay Silver ring
sizing paper or
non-porous paper

Art Clay Silver, 20 grams

Art Clay Silver, syringe type

Fine silver wire, 5 cm

Ammonite fossil

Metal clay release agent

Bench tool kit, page 9

Soldering kit, page 9

Work mat

Spacers, 1.5 mm

Roller

Craft knife

Embossing heat gun

Wire mesh for drying

Oven, preheated to 285°F
(140°C)

Round form for doming

Kiln, preheated to 1470°F
(800°C)

Cling film

Paintbrush

Clay shaper

FINISHED SIZE
2.5 x 2 x 1 cm

▶▶▶ Go

1. Determine the desired ring size, and add two sizes to allow for clay shrinkage. Wrap a piece of ring sizing paper on a ring mandrel at this size.

2. Remove the silver clay from its package, and place it on a work mat prepared with release agent. Using 1.5-mm spacers and a roller, roll out the clay, folding it lengthwise until you have a strip that is ½ inch (1.3 cm) wide. Trim the clay to the width you want, and drape it over the ring sizing paper.

3. Wrap the clay strip around the mandrel, letting the excess clay overlap itself. With a craft knife or tissue blade, cut through the center of the overlap at a 45-degree angle. Remove the excess clay.

4. Use your thumb to taper one of the edges to the mandrel. Use the syringe to apply a generous amount of slip on top of the tapered edge. Wrap the other end of the clay around until it overlaps the syringed slip. Trim any excess clay, and apply gentle pressure to the seam for a few seconds to ensure a strong joint. Extrude more slip from the syringe to fill in the seam.

5. Dry the ring with an embossing heat gun for two minutes. Slide the ring off the mandrel, and carefully remove the paper. If necessary, fill in the seam on the inside of the ring, and fill in any other cracks with slip. Put the ring on wire mesh, and place it into the preheated oven to dry.

6. Prepare the ammonite fossil with release agent. Work four grams of silver clay into a ball. Press the clay into the fossil, and form a disk that is approximately 1 mm thick.

Prepare the doming form with release agent, and shape the clay disk onto the form. Dry the disk with a heat gun for two minutes, remove the domed disk, and place into the oven (with the ring) to dry.

7. Cut about fifteen 1-mm to 3-mm lengths of fine silver wire. Place each wire on a soldering block, and ball with the torch.

8. Remove the disk and the ring from the oven, and sand both pieces. Place the ring back on the mandrel. Using a syringe, extrude several flowing lines of clay all around the ring. Dry the clay with a heat gun.

9. Flatten the ring joint with sandpaper, and apply a generous amount of slip to the area. Join the disk to the ring by applying pressure.

10. Extrude a small amount of slip from the syringe under one side of the disk. Use tweezers to place the fine silver balls into the slip. Use a damp paintbrush to tidy up any clay. Repeat on the other side of the disk. Place the ring on wire mesh, and dry it with a heat gun for five minutes.

11. Place the ring into the hot, preheated kiln, and fire for five minutes. Remove the ring from the kiln, quench, and brush with a soft brass brush. Burnish the ring to finish it.

Want to Make Another Ring?

Texture the metal clay band with a texture sheet or add a cubic zirconia to the center of the fossil-printed clay for a little added sparkle.

►► ▶ Get Set

Sterling silver round wire,
12 gauge, 9 inches
(22.9 cm)

Sterling silver round wire,
18 gauge, 1½ inches
(3.8 cm)

White diamond, round cut,
2.3 mm

Bench tool kit, page 9

Soldering kit, page 9

FINISHED SIZE
2.5 x 5.1 x 4.4 cm

►► ▶ ▶ Go

1. Use wire snips to cut the 12-gauge silver wire into seven pieces, varying each length from 1 inch (2.5 cm) to 1¼ inches (3.2 cm). Use round-nose pliers to bend the cut wire pieces into circles.

2. Place the wire circles on a soldering block. Fuse each wire circle into a complete ring with a torch. Heat the silver slowly, and move the flame often so the metal skin crawls and puckers into an organic form.

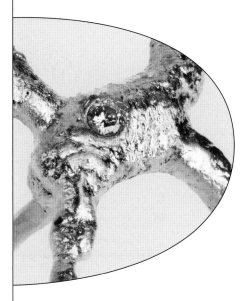

3. Use tweezers to position the cooled rings in a circular pattern on the soldering block. Make sure each ring is touching two other rings.

4. With the torch on high, pass the flame over all the rings to heat them evenly. Once the rings are near the fusing point, lower the heat and focus on fusing the individual rings to one another. Continue until all seven rings are fused together.

5. With tweezers, turn the fused piece over while it's still hot. Set up the 18-gauge wire vertically with a third hand so one end is touching the place where you would like to start the ring band. Fuse the wire to the back of the piece. Pickle, rinse, and dry. Brass brush the metal.

6. Gypsy set the diamond in an area that is deep enough to accommodate the height of the stone.

7. Bend the ring shank into a circle shape with a pair of round-nose pliers, making a ring with an adjustable shank.

**SAWING • RETICULATION • SOLDERING • FINISHING • FORMING
DRILLING • RIVETING • ADDING A PATINA**

➤➤ ➤ **Get Set**

Sterling silver sheet,
   16 gauge, 2¾ x ½ inch
   (7 x 1.3 cm)

Sterling silver round wire,
   16 gauge, ¼ inch
   (6 mm)

Bench tool kit, page 9

Soldering kit, page 9

Liver of sulfur

FINISHED SIZE
Band, 1.2 to 0.5 cm wide

➤➤ ➤ **Go**

1. Calculate the length of silver sheet needed to make the desired size ring. Add 1.5 to 2 cm to this length to allow for the overlapping ends. Mark the outline of the ring band on the 16-gauge sterling silver sheet, tapering the strip's width from 1.2 cm to 0.5 cm.

2. Saw the strip from the silver sheet, and file the edges smooth. Place the strip on a soldering block, and reticulate its wide end using a bushy torch flame. Brass brush the strip.

3. Decide which side of the reticulation you want to feature. File the other side of the reticulated area smooth. Sand the ring to an 800-grit finish, and polish to a rouge shine.

4. Use half-round pliers to form the strip into a ring, making sure the smooth tapered end of the band rests on top of the wide

reticulated end. Place the band on a ring mandrel, and hammer it round using a plastic mallet. (The tapered end of the band should be touching the wide end.)

5. Drill a 1.2-mm hole through both layers of metal. Use a round burr to remove the inside edge of each hole. Rivet the tapered end to the wide end with a short length of 16-gauge silver wire on a ring mandrel. Make sure the ring is still the desired size. File and sand the rivet head from the inside and the outside of the ring, creating a hidden rivet.

6. Use a liver-of-sulfur solution to patina the reticulated area. Polish the ring again, making sure to remove any marks indicating the rivet.

Want To Make Another Ring?

Rather than reticulating the silver, try using hardened steel punches and stamps, a textured hammer, or a rolling mill to impart a rough texture on the ring band.

DESIGNER: **SHIRLEE GRUND**

**USING A DISK CUTTER • STAMPING • CUTTING WITH METAL SHEARS
FILING • SOLDERING • FORMING • FINISHING • ADDING A PATINA**

▶ ▶ Get Set

**Copper sheet, 18 gauge,
¾ inch (1.9 cm) square**

**Sterling silver sheet,
18 gauge, 1½ x ⅜ inch
(3.8 x 1 cm)**

**Sterling silver round wire,
12 gauge, 2.5 inches
(6.4 cm)**

Bench tool kit, page 9

Soldering tool kit, page 9

**Center punch or
stamping tools**

Liver of sulfur

**FINISHED SIZE
2.5 x 2 x 1.7 cm**

▶ ▶ ▶ Go

1. Use a disk cutter to cut a ½-inch (1.3 cm) circle from the copper sheet.

2. Stamp a random dotted design on the copper disk using a center punch, hammer, and a rubber bench block or phone book. Start stamping near the center of the disk and work towards the edge.

3. Use metal shears to cut the silver sheet into a rough rectangle, approximately 1½ x ⅜ inch (3.8 x 1 cm). True the shorter ends with a file, and bring them flush together into a bezel shape.

4. Determine and cut the proper length of the 12-gauge round wire for your desired ring size. True the ends with a file, and bring them flush together into a band.

5. Solder the joints of band and the bezel. Pickle, rinse, and dry both pieces. Use a mallet and a ring mandrel to form the band and the bezel into perfect circles. Sand the top and bottom edges of the bezel smooth.

6. Mark two points on the bottom edge of the bezel that are directly across from each other (180 degrees). Make an indentation at each point with a round needle file. Make sure the band fits snugly into these indentions.

7. Use a third hand to hold the band in place on the bezel, and solder these pieces together. Pickle, rinse, and dry the ring.

8. Place a cushion over the jaws of the vise to protect the metal ring. Secure the ring in the vise so the jaws support the bezel from underneath. Using a dapping punch and hammer, flare the top edge of the bezel.

9. Solder the copper disk inside the bezel. Pickle, rinse, and dry the ring. Sand all edges smooth and round.

10. Use a liver-of-sulfur solution to patina the copper disk. Rub the silver ring with steel wool.

Want To Make Another Ring?

You can also use stamping tools or a rolling mill to create a texture on the copper disk.

Have Time To Spare?

Add a splash of color to the copper disk with torch-fired enamels.

⮕► Get Set

**Sterling silver sheet,
20 gauge, 1½ x 1½
inches (3.8 x 3.8 cm)**

**Sterling silver rectangle
wire, 1 x 4 mm, 2 inches
(5.1 cm)**

**Photocopied design
template ❶**

Bench tool kit, page 9

Soldering kit, page 9

Liver of sulfur

**FINISHED SIZE
3.3 x 2.8 x 2.3 cm**

DESIGNER'S NOTE
Other texture options
include stamping, reticulation, and roller printing.

►►► Go

1. Using the photocopied template and
a scribe, transfer the shape onto the silver
sheet. Saw out the shape. File and sand the
rough edges to a 600-grit finish.

2. Hammer the silver shape with a texturing
hammer on a steel block. With the textured
side of the silver facing down, dome the
shape with a dapping block and punch.
Using a rawhide mallet and a steel block,
flatten the edges ¼ inch (6 mm) without
losing the hammered texture.

3. Drill a hole in the center of the textured
silver shape, and pierce out an interior circle
with a saw. Saw four "cracks" that extend out
from the pierced circle.

4. Determine the shank length for your
desired ring size. Cut a piece of 1 x 4-mm
rectangular wire to this measurement.
Bend the wire into a U-shape around a ring
mandrel. File the ends of the wire even.

5. Solder the ring shank onto the concave
side of the domed silver shape. Pickle, rinse,
and dry the metal.

6. Patina the ring with a liver-of-sulfur
solution. Buff the ring with extra fine steel
wool to remove excess patina, leaving a dark
finish in the recesses.

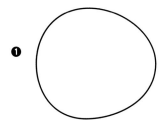

❶

▶▶ Get Set

Copper pipe, ¾ inch
(1.9 cm) in diameter,
or coupling, 1 inch
(2.5 cm) in diameter

Fine silver wire, 20 gauge,
12 inches (30.5 cm)

Bench tool kit, page 9

Soldering kit, page 9

Pipe cutter, optional

FINISHED SIZE
Size 5½, if using
copper pipe
Size 6¾ to 7½, if
using coupling

DESIGNER'S NOTE
Instead of copper pipe, you
can use copper or silver
washers. Anneal and ham-
mer the washers on a ring
mandrel to form the band.

▶▶▶ Go

1. Using a tube cutter or a jeweler's saw, cut a ¼-inch (6 mm) length of copper pipe. This is the band.

2. Sand or file the edges of the band so they are wavy. Use a planishing hammer to texture the band.

3. Divide the band into 16 sections along the centerline, and mark these locations with a permanent marker. Indent each mark with a center punch, and drill each indention with a 1-mm bit. Sand the band to a 400-grit finish.

4. Cut 16 pieces of 20-gauge fine silver wire, each ¾ inch (1.9 cm) long. (Longer wires will produce larger balls.) Ball up one end of each wire with a torch, using slightly less than half the length of each wire.

5. Hold the band in a third hand. Thread one wire through a hole in the band, with the ball on the inside of the band. Use the torch to ball the remaining wire, making sure to melt the ball close to the band. Rotate the band in the third hand, and repeat this step with each wire. Pickle the ring.

6. Tumble the ring with stainless steel shot to polish its surface.

→ Get Ready

SAWING • SCORING AND BENDING • FILING • SOLDERING • RIVETING

▶ ▶ ▶ Get Set

Sterling silver sheet,
16 gauge, 1¼ x 2¾
inches (3.2 x 7 cm)

Photocopied design
template ❶

Ebony wood, 4 x 8 cm

Bench tool kit, page 9

Soldering kit, page 9

FINISHED SIZE
Ring, 3 x 2.7 cm; with bar,
3.8 x 7.5 cm

DESIGNER'S NOTE
To create color variations,
use a different wood,
acrylic, or any material
you wish.

▶ ▶ ▶ Go

1. Use a saw to cut a piece of 16-gauge sterling silver sheet to 1¹⁄₁₆ x 2¾ inches (2.8 x 7 cm). File the edges to right angles.

2. Sand one side of the silver sheet flat on 220-grit sandpaper. Use a scribe to transfer the template onto the metal. Drill a small hole on the inside of both circles. Saw out each circle, following the inside of the scribed line.

3. Use a scribe to score the two dotted lines so they become deeper. It is important that both of these lines remain parallel and at right angles to the outer edge. With a triangular needle file, deepen the grooves until they are deep enough to see a line on the reverse side of the sheet metal. Use a square needle file to broaden these grooves and create 90-degree channels.

4. Fold the sheet at the grooves, making two 90-degree bends and making the two finger holes line up. Solder the bends with medium solder. Pickle, rinse, and dry the metal.

5. Use a half-round file to align the finger holes. File the curved section of the ring,

making sure each side of the curve is even with the other.

6. Give the ring a final finish and texture, making sure to remove all firescale. Polish all edges of the ring.

7. Using a saw, cut a piece of ebony that is 4.5 x 4.5 mm and 1.5 inches (3.8 cm) long. Ensure that the ebony fits snugly between the parallel plates of the ring, resting in the U-channel. Finish the wood with 320-grit sandpaper, and carefully file all edges with a flat file so they are not sharp.

8. Use a 1.2-mm bit to drill two holes on the top metal sheet, then two holes on the bottom. (Refer to the project photo for hole placement.) Insert the ebony so it sticks out 4 mm from the straight edge. Carefully drill two holes through the wood, using the top two holes on the metal as a guide.

9. De-burr the drill holes and insert the 16-gauge sterling silver round wire. Snip the wire so it protrudes 1 mm on each side. Rivet the wire using a chasing hammer. Repeat for the other side.

10. Finish the rivets using a fine hollow punch that fits just over the rivet head but doesn't touch the base sheet. Rotate the tool while tapping with a chasing hammer. Burnish the edges of the ring.

❶

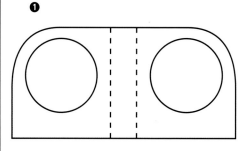

▶▶ Get Set

Sterling silver round wire, 14 gauge, 2½ inches (6.4 cm)

Copper tubing, 2 mm OD, ¼ inch (0.6 cm)

Scraps of colored tin

Paper clips

Bench tool kit, page 9

Soldering kit, page 9

Hydraulic press or vise

2 rubber pieces

2 steel plates

Inner tube rubber

FINISHED SIZE
2.5 x 3 x 1.2 cm

DESIGNER'S NOTE
To determine the proper length of silver wire for the ring shank, measure your size with a ring gauge, and press the ring onto a piece of paper to leave a faint indentation. Draw on the indentation so you have a circle, then draw a straight line across the top of the circle, and then draw two straight lines, one on each side of the circle. This U-shape is the template for your ring size.

▶▶▶ Go

1. Determine and cut the proper length of the 14-gauge wire for your desired ring size. Bend the wire around a ring mandrel to form a U-shape. File the ends of the wire flat.

2. Cut two lengths of copper tubing, each 3 mm long. Solder one length to each end of the silver U, with the opening facing up. Pickle, rinse, and dry the metal.

3. Mark three rectangles on the back of the colored tin: make the bottom layer 2.8 x 1.1 mm; make the middle layer 3.2 x 1.1 mm; and make the top layer 2.8 x 1.3 mm. Cut out each rectangle with scissors, rounding the corners as you go. File off any burrs.

4. Using template ❶ as a guide, make a squiggle shape out of a paper clip with round-nose pliers. Use masking tape to secure the paper clip to the back of the middle layer of tin so that only the vertical lines of the squiggle are making contact with the tin.

❶

5. Place the tin and the wire squiggle between two pieces of rubber and sandwich them between two steel plates. Press the stack in a hydraulic press or in the jaws of a vise.

6. Following the same process described in step 5, press-form the top layer of tin with a straight piece of wire placed horizontally along the rectangle.

7. Using the ring shank as a guide, mark the hole placements on the bottom tin sheet layer. Punch and drill these two holes with a 2-mm bit. Using these holes as a guide, drill matching holes in the middle and top layers of the tin.

8. Cover the jaws of your vise with inner tube rubber. Secure the ring shank in the vise with 5 mm of the shank protruding.

9. Thread the three tin pieces onto the ring shank. Flare the tubes with the center punch, and finish the tube rivet with the round face of a chasing hammer.

Want To Make Another Ring?

Use a circle shape for the tin instead of a rectangle, or cut windows in the tin to reveal the colors of the sheet below.

▶▶ Get Set

Sterling silver round wire, 22 gauge, 2 inches (5.1 cm)

Sterling silver square wire, 10 gauge, 2¼ inches (5.7 cm)

Copper disk, 22 gauge, ½ inch (1.3 cm) in diameter

Copper sheet, 22 gauge, ¾ x ½ inch (1.9 x 1.3 cm)

Bench tool kit, page 9

Soldering kit, page 9

Kiln

Enamels, Etruscan blue and tangerine

Particulate respirator

Safety glasses

Metal cleaner

Artist paintbrushes, size 2

Firescale inhibitor

Enamel adhesive

Enamel sifter, 100 mesh

Stainless steel firing trivet

Stainless steel mesh firing rack

Stainless steel firing fork

Heat-resistant surface

Liver of sulfur

FINISHED SIZE
2.5 x 2.2 x 0.8 cm

▶▶▶ Go

1. Measure, mark, and cut the 10-gauge square wire to the proper length for the desired ring size. File both ends of the wire.

2. Anneal the square wire. Bend the wire ends together with parallel pliers, and solder them closed. Pickle, rinse, and dry the ring band.

3. On the side of the ring, center punch a divot in the center of the solder seam. Drill a hole at this point with a 1.7-mm bit. Sand both sides and the interior of the ring with 280-grit sandpaper. Make sure the edges are not sharp.

4. Measure, mark, and cut a ¾ x ½-inch (1.9 x 1.3 cm) rectangle from the 22-gauge copper sheet. Straighten the edges and round the corners with a flat file.

5. Using the project photo as a guide, mark and drill two 1.5-mm holes on the copper rectangle and disk.

6. Sand both surfaces of the copper pieces. Dip the copper pieces in metal cleaner, rinse, and dry. Coat one surface of the copper pieces with the firescale-inhibiting compound. Let dry. Brush enamel adhesive on the other side of the copper pieces.

7. Hold the copper circle on the tip of your finger. Sift the Etruscan blue enamel onto the surface to a depth of 3 mm. Carefully place the circle on a firing trivet and then place the trivet on the mesh firing rack. Repeat this step with the copper rectangle and the tangerine enamel. Fire the enamel and let the pieces air cool. Sand the copper surfaces.

8. Use your fingers to loosely bend the 22-gauge silver wire in half. Thread the wire ends through the holes in the blue circle, and then through the holes in the tangerine rectangle.

9. Thread the ends of the silver wire through opposite sides of the hole in the ring shank. Using two pairs of pliers, grip the ends of the wire, and carefully and firmly pull the wire tight. Bend the wires counterclockwise up and over the ring shank and below the copper rectangle. Snip the wire, leaving just enough length to tuck the ends back into the hole in the ring shank.

10. Use fine steel wool or a fine fiber wheel to texture the ring shank. Do not scratch the enamel surface.

Want to Make Another Ring?

Change the color or the shape of the enameled components.

Have Time to Spare?

Add another enameled layer to the ring, or add a pearl to the wire before threading the enameled pieces onto the band.

DESIGNER: **COLLEEN BARAN**

▶ ▶ **Get Set**

**Sterling silver sheet,
20 gauge, 1 x 1 inch
(2.5 x 2.5 cm)**

**Sterling silver round wire,
14 gauge, 3 inches
(7.6 cm)**

**Embroidery thread, 6 feet
(1.8 meters)**

**Photocopied design
template ❶**

Bench tool kit, page 9

Soldering kit, page 9

**Disk cutter, ⅞-inch
(2.2 cm) diameter**

Fine beading needle

**FINISHED SIZE
2.5 x 2.2 x 2.2 cm**

▶ ▶ ▶ **Go**

1. Using the disk cutter, cut out a ⅞-inch (2.2 cm) disk from the sterling silver sheet. Use the template to mark the placement of the drill holes. Drill each marked spot with a 1-mm bit. Sand the silver disk. Use a round burr to clean up the sharp edges of each hole on both sides of the silver disk. (This prevents the fraying of the embroidery thread.)

2. To make the band, saw the 14-gauge silver wire to the proper length for your desired ring size. Bend the wire into a band, and solder the ends together. Place the band on a ring mandrel, and hammer the band with a rawhide mallet.

3. Cut a 1-mm piece of 14-gauge round wire to use as a post for the silver disk. Solder one end of the post to the ring and the other end of the post to the silver disk.

4. File and sand any tool marks, solder blobs, or rough edges off the ring. Wearing proper safety equipment, give a light polish to the ring with the flexible shaft and rubber wheels.

❶

5. Thread the 6-foot (1.8 m) strand of embroidery thread through the eye of the beading needle. Beginning at the center row, start by feeding the needle through the "odd" hole that is sandwiched between the equally spaced ones. Feed the needle with the knot right side up. (This knot will be hidden under the sewn "stone" later.)

6. On the underside of the ring, thread the needle through the next hole over. Pull the needle through to the top of the disk. Put the next stitch through its "opposite" hole in the first row. (To be sure it's the right hole, you can count on either side to find the middle.) Once this first stitch is made, move over to the next hole and repeat. Stitch around the circle using the same process. Occasionally smooth out the thread to prevent it from twisting and bunching.

7. Once the first row is completed, move onto the middle rows, and finally the outer rows, stitching in the same pattern. When the last hole is sewn, knot the thread under the silver disk, and snip off any excess.

Want to Make Another Ring?

Use variegated thread for a multicolored look, or shiny thread or soft, fluffy wool for a different texture.

Have Time to Spare?

Drill more holes to add extra height and dimension to the thread.

⇛ ▶ **Get Set**

Sterling silver sheet,
18 gauge, 2¾ inches
(7 cm)

Sterling silver round wire,
14 gauge, 2 inches
(5.1 cm)

Fine silver wire, 26 gauge,
8 inches (20.3 cm)

Beads of your choice,
8 mm

Bench tool kit, page 9

Soldering kit, page 9

FINISHED SIZE
3 x 2.5 x 0.8 cm

DESIGNER'S NOTE
Buy a pre-made sterling silver band in any width to save time.

⇛ ▶ ▶ **Go**

1. Determine the length of metal needed for your desired ring size. Saw an 8-mm strip of the 18-gauge silver sheet to this measurement. File the edges and square the ends of the strip.

2. Bring the ends of the strip together with pliers, and solder the joint. Pickle, rinse, and dry the band. Place the band on a ring mandrel and use a plastic mallet to hammer the band round. File and sand the solder joint.

3. Use chain-nose pliers to bend the 14-gauge wire into an arc approximately ½ inch (1.3 cm) wide and ¼ inch (6 mm) tall. File the wire ends flat so they fit snugly against the ring band.

4. On top of a soldering block, use a third hand and cross-locking tweezers to hold the wire arc centered on top of the ring band. Solder the arc in place. Pickle, rinse, and dry.

5. Polish the ring with a flexible shaft attachment or a brass brush.

6. Cut the 26-gauge fine silver wire into nine 3-inch (7.6 cm) pieces. Ball up the end of each wire with a torch.

7. Thread a bead onto a balled wire, make a loop at the end, and attach it to the arc on the ring band. Wrap the wire tail back around the wire at the base of the bead, and snip off any extra length. Repeat with each bead.

Want To Make Another Ring?

Use a mix of beads, such as wood with pearls, round and faceted beads, or earth tones with bright colors. Use different sized beads for extra dimension.

Have Time To Spare?

Add texture to the band with a hammer or cylinder burr.

▶ ▶ **Get Set**

Sterling silver bezel wire,
    28 gauge, ³⁄₁₆ inch
    (5 mm) tall, 2¾ inches
    (7 cm)

Sterling silver sheet,
    24 gauge, 1 ⅛ x ¾ inch
    (2.8 x 1.9 cm)

Sterling silver flat wire,
    4 x 2 mm, 2½ inches
    (6.4 cm)

30 to 40 beads, each
    4 to 5 mm

Bench tool kit, page 9

Soldering kit, page 9

Plumber's putty

FINISHED SIZE
Top element, 2.8 x 1.9 cm

▶ ▶ ▶ **Go**

1. Use your fingers to form the bezel wire into an oval. Solder the ends of the oval together. Pickle and rinse the oval. Sand the solder joint, and sand the bezel flat on the top and bottom edges.

2. Place the bezel on the 24-gauge silver sheet. Draw an oval on the silver sheet that is 1 to 2 mm larger than the bezel. Saw the oval shape out of the silver sheet, and file the edges.

3. Position the bezel on the silver oval and solder these pieces together. Pickle, rinse, and dry the metal.

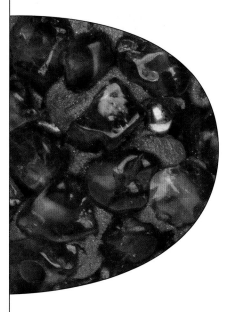

4. Measure and saw the flat wire to the proper length for your desired ring size. Bend the band with chain-nose pliers so the ends meet. Solder the band together then pickle and rinse it.

5. Hammer the ring band on a ring mandrel to make it completely round. File and sand the ring band.

6. Center the ring band on the back of the bezel plate and position it so the long side of the oval will sit vertically on your finger. Solder the band to the bezel. Pickle, rinse, and completely dry the ring.

7. Mix a ½-inch (1.3 cm) ball of plumber's putty until it's a consistent color. Pack the putty into the bezel setting, forming a uniform cabochon shape.

8. Place the 4- to 5-mm beads into a small dish. Roll the top of the putty cabochon into the beads until the desired coverage is achieved. Let the putty harden completely.

9. Rub the metal with steel wool to finish the ring.

Want To Make Another Ring?

Alter the shape of the bezel or set a variety of beads in the putty.

►► Get Set

Silver metal clay, 6 grams
or less

Sterling silver round wire,
14 to 11 gauge,
2¾ inches (7 cm)

Bench tool kit, page 9

Soldering kit, page 9

Forming armature, such
as light bulb or plastic
Easter egg

Rolling tool

Playing cards

Texture material

Nonstick surface

Olive oil or lubricating balm

Liver of sulfur

Acrylic paint, off white

Paintbrush

FINISHED SIZE
Ring top, 2.5 cm

DESIGNER'S NOTE
To achieve the ragged edges
of the metal clay element,
use clay that is slightly dry.
There is a perfect point
where the clay will take texture but will crack around the
edges. If working with a fresh
package of clay, roll a ball
in your hands to dry it out.
Alternately, use files, emery
boards, and sandpaper to
distress the edges of the dry,
formed element.

►►► Go

1. Roll a peanut-sized ball of silver metal clay. Be sure to compress it to remove any air pockets or fold lines.

2. Use a rolling tool to flatten the ball to the thickness of four playing cards. Roll slightly in one direction until you form an oval, then roll fully in the other direction to achieve a more rounded shape. Place the circle of clay onto a lightly lubricated texture surface, and re-roll the clay to the thickness of three playing cards.

3. Place the clay circle, textured side down, on a lubricated forming armature (light bulb). (A small circle dried on a large form will create a relatively flat dish. A larger circle dried on a smaller form will create a relatively deep bowl.) Let the clay air dry or place the armature in a dehydrator.

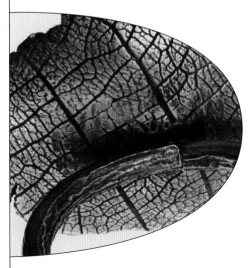

4. While the metal clay is drying, form the sterling silver round wire into a band of the desired size. Solder the joint. Pickle, rinse, and dry the band. Texture the sterling silver band with a hammer. File a flat spot on the band at the soldered seam.

5. Make sure the metal clay is completely dry. Sand a flat area centered on the bottom of the dome.

6. Torch fire the metal clay dome on a soldering block for 4 to 7 minutes. Wire brush the metal clay element, and burnish the flat spot.

7. Place the dome on a soldering block. Hold the band in cross-locking tweezers so the flat spot on the band rests on the flat spot on the dome. Solder the dome and band together. Pickle and rinse the ring.

8. Wire brush the ring, and then patina it with a liver-of-sulfur solution. Use a polishing pad to remove the patina from the shank, allowing the texture to be highlighted.

9. Brush acrylic paint inside the domed portion of the metal clay element. Allow the paint to dry for about 10 seconds, then use a slightly damp paper towel to wipe away the paint, leaving it in the recessed areas of the textured pattern.

> ▶ Get Ready

USING A DISK CUTTER • SANDING • BENDING • SOLDERING • FINISHING

▶ ▶ Get Set

Sterling silver sheet,
   22 gauge, ½ inch
   (1.3 cm)

Sterling silver square wire,
   2 x 2 mm, 2½ inches
   (6.4 cm)

Bench tool kit, page 9

Soldering kit, page 9

FINISHED SIZE
2.3 x 2 x 1 cm

▶ ▶ ▶ Go

1. Use a disk cutter to cut a 14.2-mm circle from the 22-gauge sterling silver sheet. Punch an 8-mm hole inside the 14.2-mm circle, slightly off center.

2. Flatten the silver "washer" with a mallet on a steel block. Sand the washer by hand using a circular motion. Anneal the washer. Pickle, rinse, and dry it.

3. Using round-nose pliers, bend and twist the silver washer at its narrowest point.

4. Measure and cut the square wire to the proper length for your desired ring size. Anneal the wire and pickle it.

5. Use half-round pliers to bend the wire into a ring shape. Solder the ends of the ring closed. Pickle, rinse, and dry the ring.

6. Place the ring on a ring mandrel, and shape it with a mallet. Flatten the ring by hammering it between two steel blocks. Sand both sides of the ring using a circular motion.

7. Mark where the twisted washer will sit on the ring band. Use a jeweler's saw to cut the ring at an angle so the curved washer will fit nicely on the band. Use a file to make the fit perfect.

8. Rest the twisted washer upside down on a soldering block. Hold the ring shank in place with cross-locking tweezers, and solder the two parts together.

9. Brass brush the ring to finish it.

►► Get Set

Sterling silver square wire,
    12 gauge, 9½ inches
    (24.13 cm)

Bench tool kit, page 9

Soldering kit, page 9

Diamond burr

FINISHED SIZE
3.5 x 2.5 x 1 cm

►►► Go

1. Using wire cutters, cut the sterling silver square wire into four pieces, each 2¼ inches (6 cm) long. Bend the wires around a bracelet mandrel or other large round form with your fingers, and lightly tap them with a rawhide mallet to create a slight arc.

2. File the ends of two wires so they will fit together flush and form a marquise shape. Repeat with the second pair of wires. Solder the two sets of curved wires together. Pickle, rinse, and dry the metal.

3. File one end point on each marquise wire shape slightly flat. Solder the two marquise shapes together at these flattened points. Pickle, rinse, and dry. Sand off any solder or surface flaws with a sanding stick.

4. Use your fingers and light taps with a rawhide mallet to bend the new wire form around a ring mandrel, making a U-shape and keeping the joint where the two marquises meet at the center point.

5. Keeping the ring on the mandrel, use round-nose pliers to curl the end points under and create a graceful curve. As you curl the ends under, pull the ring further around the mandrel. Carefully use round-nose pliers to finish any additional shaping, making sure not to mar the metal.

6. Sand the inside and outside of the ring to remove any surface flaws and create a sleek, smooth finish.

7. Use a diamond burr attachment in the flexible shaft to evenly texture the inside edge of the square wire.

8. Polish the front and back of the ring to a high shine with a muslin wheel on the flexible shaft. Clean off any polishing compound in an ultrasonic cleaner or with soapy water.

DESIGNER: **DANIELLE MILLER-GILLIAM**

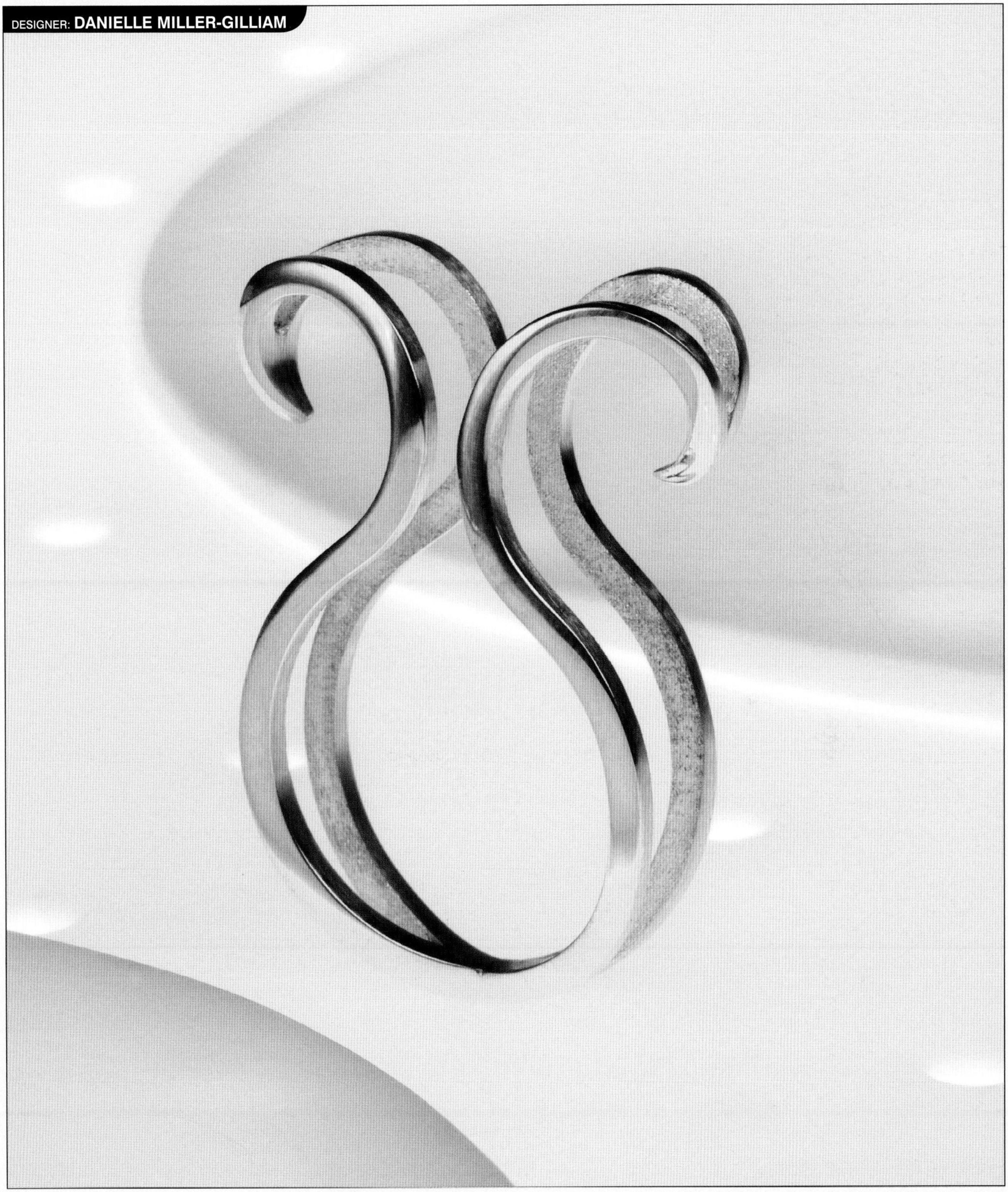

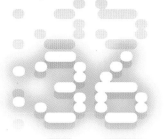

SAWING • FILING • USING A DISK CUTTER • TEXTURING • SOLDERING FORMING • HAMMERING • ADDING A PATINA

►► Get Set

Sterling silver charm blank, flat

Brass sheet, floral pattern, 24 gauge, 1 inch (2.5 cm) square

Sterling silver round wire, 14 gauge, 2¾ inches (7 cm)

Bench tool kit, page 9

Soldering tool kit, page 9

Brass antique black patina

FINISHED SIZE 1.6 x 2 cm

DESIGNER'S NOTE
If floral is not your style, try a smooth disk, and texture the charm with a hammered finish for contrast.

►►► Go

1. If the charm has a loop for attaching a jump ring, remove it with a jeweler's saw. File the charm smooth with a metal file. Center the charm on the disk-cutting block at the ⅜-inch (1 cm) hole. Use a brass head mallet to punch out the circle.

2. Use a disk cutter to cut a ½-inch (1.3 cm) circle from the brass sheet.

3. Use a center punch and a brass hammer to add dots around the perimeter of the charm. If the charm becomes distorted, use a plastic mallet and bench block to flatten it.

4. Melt solder on the flat area near the edge of the inner circle of the charm. Flux the textured side of the brass circle, and place it on the open hole of the silver charm with the textured side down. Re-heat the piece to solder the brass to the silver. Pickle, rinse, and dry the metal.

5. Determine the length of metal needed for a half size smaller than the desired ring size. Cut the 14-gauge wire to this measurement. File the wire ends flat, and shape the wire so that the ends meet without a gap. Solder the joint together. Pickle, rinse, and dry the band.

6. Shape the band on a ring mandrel with a plastic mallet. Use a chasing hammer to texture the wire and stretch the band to the desired size.

7. Melt a small piece of easy solder in the center of the back of the brass circle. Use cross-locking tweezers to hold the band in place on the melted solder. Re-melt the solder to join the band to the charm. Pickle, rinse, and dry the ring.

8. Patina the ring using a liver-of-sulfur solution. Rub the ring with steel wool in a circular motion to remove the top layer of patina, revealing the floral pattern.

DESIGNER: **CYNTHIA DEL GIUDICE**

CUTTING METAL · SANDING · SHAPING · SOLDERING
ADDING A HEAT PATINA

►► ► Get Set

Copper sheet, 26 gauge,
   1½ inches (4 cm) square

Sterling silver wire,
   12 gauge, 2¾ inches
   (7 cm)

Bench tool kit, page 9

Soldering kit, page 9

Thick felt

FINISHED SIZE
4 x 2 x 1.5 cm

DESIGNER'S NOTE
The thin copper sheet
is easy to form, but its
final structure makes a
strong shape.

►► ► Go

1. Use scissors to cut a 1½-inch (3.8 cm) square from the copper sheet. Round the corners, and sand the edges with 220-grit sandpaper.

2. Anneal the copper to soften the metal for ease in shaping.

3. With round-nose pliers, form an initial center curl in the copper sheet. Freely bend and twist the remaining copper around this center curl into a multi-petal rose shape. Bend the petals outward from the center curl with round-nose pliers.

4. Place the rose upside down on thick felt to protect the petals. Hammer the bottom carefully to make a small flat surface.

5. Depending on the ring size desired, snip the 12-gauge sterling silver wire to the proper length. Shape the ring with chain-nose pliers, and solder the joint. Pickle and rinse the ring. Place it on a ring mandrel, and hammer the ring with a mallet to make the ring completely round.

6. With the rose resting upside down on a soldering block, melt a small amount of easy solder on the flat hammered spot. Hold the ring in place on the rose using cross-locking tweezers. Solder the ring to the band. Pickle, rinse, and dry.

7. Rub the ring with a green scrub pad or steel wool for a brushed finish. Add a patina to the copper with gentle heat from the torch.

Want to Make Another Ring?

Instead of a copper rose, make one from sterling silver or brass.

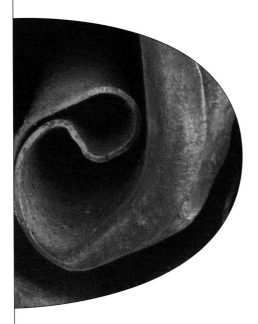

➤ ▶ Get Set

Sterling silver square wire ring band in desired size, 1.25 mm

Sterling silver round wire, 18 gauge, 1¼ inches (3.2 cm)

Sterling silver disk, 20 gauge, 1.5 cm in diameter

Photocopied design template ❶

Bench tool kit, page 9

Soldering kit, page 9

FINISHED SIZE
5.9 x 2 x 1.1 cm

▶ ▶ ▶ Go

1. Using a 1-mm bit, drill a small dimple in the center of the top of the ring blank.

2. With a torch, ball one end of the 18-gauge sterling silver wire.

3. Find and mark the center of the 1.5-cm silver disk. Drill a 1-mm hole at the marked point. Use the photocopied template to transfer the design onto the disk. Saw out the flower design. File and sand all edges.

4. Use a dapping block and punch to slightly dome the silver flower. Thread the flower onto the 18-gauge wire, 8 mm from the beaded end. Solder the flower in place. Pickle, rinse, and dry the metal.

5. Hold the ring blank with cross-locking tweezers with the drilled dimple on top. Hold the 18-gauge wire with another pair of cross-locking tweezers so the base of the wire sits in the drilled dimple. Solder the wire in place on the ring.

6. Sand the wire flower "stem" with fine sandpaper, and finish it with a green scrub pad.

Want To Make Another Ring?

Use 18-karat gold for the flower.

❶

⟶ ▶ **Get Set**

Sterling silver sheet,
   16 gauge, 2½ x ³⁄₁₆ inch
   (6.4 x 0.5 cm)

Sterling silver wire,
   12 gauge, ¼ inch
   (6 mm)

Sterling silver wire,
   10 gauge, 2 inches
   (5.1 cm)

Bench tool kit, page 9

Soldering kit, page 9

Liver of sulfur

FINISHED SIZE
3.2 x 5.1 x 0.2 cm

DESIGNER'S NOTE
Experiment with different
shapes when forging.

▶ ▶ ▶ **Go**

1. Determine and cut the length of silver sheet needed for your desired ring size. File the sides of the sheet metal strip smooth and flat.

2. Use a hammer and ring mandrel to form the silver strip into the shape of a ring, making sure to file the ends flush. Solder the joint; pickle, rinse and dry. Round the ring with a rawhide hammer on a ring mandrel.

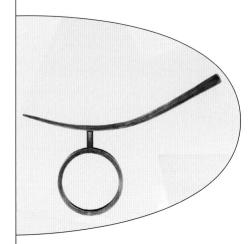

3. Drill a 3-mm hole in the top center of the ring. Solder the 12-gauge silver wire into the hole with just enough of it sticking into the middle of the ring to be able to solder it together. Pickle, rinse, and dry. File and sand the excess wire from inside the band.

4. Anneal the 10-gauge silver wire. Use a planishing hammer and bench block to forge one side of the wire one-third of the whole length. As you forge, the wire should start to gently curve to one direction. You can correct this if you want to keep the wire straight, or keep the curve as a design element. Turn the wire 45 degrees, and forge the other end.

5. Use your fingers to bend the forged wire to the desired shape. File and sand the forged wire smooth. Round the edges of the wire with a file and sandpaper.

6. Solder the forged wire to the 12-gauge wire attached to the ring. Pickle, rinse, and dry the ring.

7. Polish and patina the ring as desired to finish it.

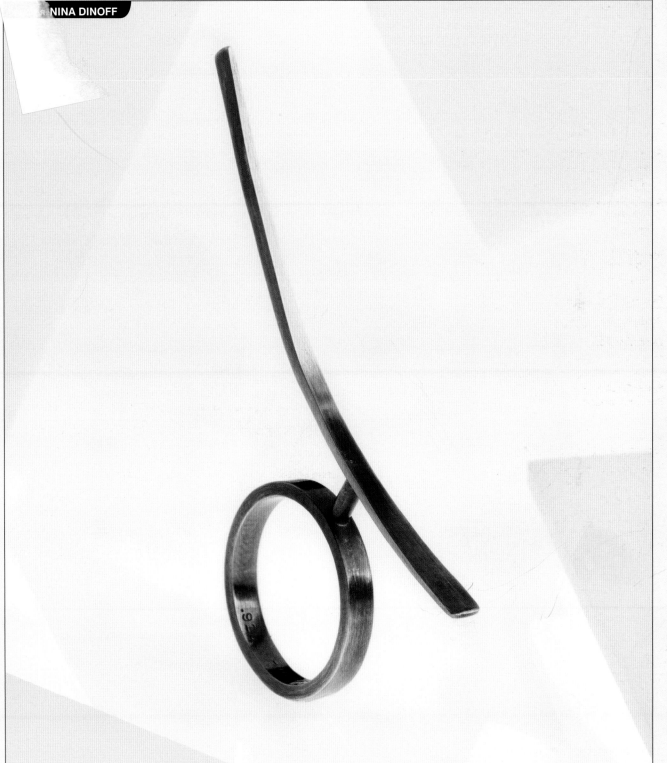

**ANNEALING • STAMPING • ROLLER PRINTING • DOMING • FILING
SOLDERING • BENDING • HAMMERING • ADDING A PATINA**

►► Get Set

Copper disk, 18 gauge,
1¼ inches (3.2 cm)
in diameter

Copper disk, 18 gauge,
¾ inch (1.9 cm)
in diameter

Sterling silver square wire,
14 gauge, 2½ inches
(6.4 cm)

Copper sheet, 22 gauge,
2 x 2½ inches
(5.1 x 6.4 cm)

Bench tool kit, page 9

Soldering kit, page 9

Texturing material, such
as aluminum grill cover
from a radiator, screen,
or tulle

Liver of sulfur

FINISHED SIZE
6.2 X 3.1 x 2.4 cm

►►► Go

1. Anneal the copper disks. Sandwich the texturing material between one copper disk and the copper sheet. Roll the stack through the rolling mill with enough pressure so it's hard to roll, but not impossible to turn. Repeat for the second copper disk.

2. Using a dapping block and punch, dome each copper disk with the textured side facing up.

3. File a small area on the back of the domed disks to make a flat surface for soldering.

4. Cut a piece of the 14-gauge square wire that is approximately 2½ inches (6.4 cm). File the edges of wire flat, and sand any burrs.

5. Use a third hand to hold the square wire, and solder one copper disk to each end of the wire.

6. Using half-round pliers, bend the square wire so the length of the wire in the center is 3 cm and the height of each end is 1.6 cm. With the flat side of a chasing hammer, hammer the ring shank on a steel block to work-harden it.

7. Patina the ring in a liver-of-sulfur solution. Use 600-grit sandpaper to rub the domed metal, removing the patina from the top of the metal but leaving the dark color in the recessed areas.

Want To Make Another Ring?

Use anything from chicken wire to tomatillo husks to add texture to the copper disks.

DESIGNER: **SIM LUTTIN**

⊳ ▶ Get Set

Sterling silver wire,
   14 gauge, 5 inches
   (13 cm)

Sterling silver wire,
   18 gauge, ⁷⁄₁₆ inch
   (1 cm)

Graphite block, 1 inch
   (2.5 cm) square

Bench tool kit, page 9

Soldering kit, page 9

Mandrel, ¹³⁄₁₆ inch
   (2.1 cm) in diameter

Two-part epoxy

FINISHED SIZE
4.6 x 2 x 1.5 cm

▶ ▶ ▶ Go

1. Wrap the 14-gauge silver wire around the ¹³⁄₁₆-inch (2.1 cm) mandrel five times, making sure to weave the wire through the layers. Adjust the ends of the wires so they meet flush. Solder the joint to make the band.

2. Using a third hand for positioning, solder the 18-gauge sterling silver wire vertically onto the seam of the band. Pickle, rinse, and dry the band.

3. Place the band on a ring mandrel, and push it down as far as it will go. Tighten the wires with your fingers to slightly work-harden the band.

4. Beginning with the corners, file the graphite block into an oval shape that measures approximately 1.5 x 2 x 1.5 cm. Create small facets on the graphite surface with a file, leaving the rough filing marks as texture.

5. Find and mark the center of the bottom of the graphite oval. Using a 1-mm bit, drill a hole 0.8 mm into the graphite at the marked point. Using two-part epoxy, secure the graphite oval to the vertical wire peg on the band.

Want To Make Another Ring?

Substitute colored acrylic for the graphite.

SAWING · FILING · FORMING JUMP RINGS · SOLDERING FINISHING · ADDING A PATINA

→ ▶ Get Set

Sterling silver round wire, 12 gauge, 1½ inches (3.8 cm)

Sterling silver round wire, 14 gauge, 3 inches (7.6 cm)

Copper rod, 6 gauge, 1⅛ inches (2.9 cm)

Bench tool kit, page 9

Soldering kit, page 9

Liver of sulfur

Sealing wax

FINISHED SIZE
3 x 2.5 cm

DESIGNER'S NOTE
This ring uses a 1½-inch (3.8 cm) piece of 12-gauge sterling silver wire to make a size 6½ ring. You'll need to adjust this length accordingly for your desired ring size. If you're making a larger ring, the copper rod will have to be longer as well.

▶ ▶ ▶ Go

1. Cut a 1½-inch (3.8 cm) piece of 12-gauge sterling silver round wire, and file the ends flat. Use a hammer to slightly flare the ends so they fit flat against the width of the 14-gauge wire.

2. Make two 14-gauge sterling silver jump rings on a 4-mm mandrel. Close the jump rings with pliers.

3. Solder one silver jump ring to each flared end of the 12-gauge wire. Pickle, rinse and dry the metal. File and sand the solder joints.

4. Use your fingers to bend the 12-gauge wire over a ring mandrel to make a U-shaped ring shank.

5. Saw 1⅛ inches (2.9 cm) of the 6-gauge copper. File the ends of the copper rod flat.

6. Slide the copper rod through the jump rings, leaving an even amount sticking out on each end. Mark the place on each side where the rod sticks out from the jump ring. Saw down the center of the copper rod in a straight line to each marked point.

7. Slide the rod through the jump rings, and flare the split rod with a chasing tool or flat screwdriver. Flip the ring over and repeat flaring on the other side. Continue flipping the rod and flaring the ends until the rod does not slide out of the jump rings. File and sand the flared rod.

8. Add a liver-of-sulfur patina to the ring, and seal it with wax.

**SAWING • FILING • SOLDERING • HAMMERING • SANDING
FORMING JUMP RINGS • POLISHING**

►► Get Set

Sterling silver square
wire, 12 gauge,
3 inches (7.6 cm)

Sterling silver round wire,
16 gauge, 2½ inches
(6.4 cm)

Sterling silver round wire,
4 gauge, ¼ inch
(6 mm)

Bench tool kit, page 9

Soldering kit, page 9

Mandrel, ⅛ inch
(3 mm) diameter

2 pairs cross-locking
tweezers

FINISHED SIZE
2.5 x 2 x .2 cm

DESIGNER'S NOTE
Use scraps to make your
dangles, or add some
beads for color.

►►► Go

1. Wrap the square wire around a ring
mandrel at the desired ring size. Be sure to
keep the wire flat against the mandrel and
tightly wind the wire using your fingers to
avoid denting. Remove the wire ring from
mandrel. Cut through one side of the wire
with a saw, perpendicular to the ring.

2. File the ends of the ring flat. Using your
fingers and flat-nose pliers, join the ends of
the ring. Solder the ring joint with hard solder.

3. Use needle files to file the joint on
the sides and inside of the square band.
Hammer the ring flat on a steel block,
and round on the ring mandrel with a
nylon hammer.

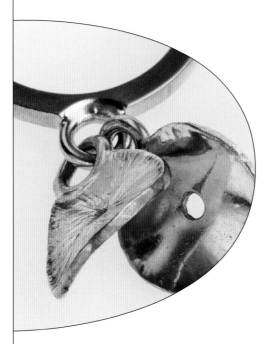

4. Use a round needle file to notch the ring
shank at its solder joint. This notch should go
three quarters of the way through the shank,
creating a "seat" for the jump ring that will
hold the dangles. Sand the ring.

5. Make several jump rings with the
16-gauge sterling silver round wire around
the ⅛-inch (3 mm) mandrel. Close one jump
ring with flat-nose and chain-nose pliers. Set
aside the remaining jump rings to use for the
decorative dangles.

6. Using a third hand and two pairs of
cross-locking tweezers, arrange the square-
wire ring and the round-wire jump ring for
soldering. Solder together using medium
solder. Pickle and rinse the ring.

7. Sand the ring to a 320-grit finish. The
completed ring shank may be textured,
polished, patinated, or even gold plated.
Polish the inside of the ring with an interior
ring buff on a polishing lathe. Use a steel
burnisher to polish all edges.

8. Make decorative dangles by: filing
4-gauge wire into a cone shape; leaving the
wire in a rod form, about 12 mm in length; or
melting scrap silver into balls and soldering
them together.

9. Solder a jump ring to each dangle with
the joint remaining open. Attach each dangle
to the ring and close the jump ring. Texture or
sand the dangles to complement the ring.

SAWING • ANNEALING • FILING • SOLDERING
SANDING • HAMMERING

►►► Get Set

Fine silver sheet, 18 gauge,
⁷⁄₁₆ x 2 ³⁄₁₆ inches
(1.1 x 6 cm)

Bench tool kit, page 9

Soldering kit, page 9

Nylon synclastic stake or
steel sinusoidal stake

Nylon hammer with narrow
shaped end

FINISHED SIZE
Size 6½ ring, 8 mm wide

►►► Go

1. Use dividers to scribe a 10-mm-wide strip on one edge of the 18-gauge fine silver sheet. Shear or saw out the strip. Cut the length to 5.8 cm for a size 6½ ring.

2. Begin shaping the strip around the anticlastic stake using the narrow end of the nylon hammer. Curve the sides into a U-shape, and form the strip into a band at the same time. Anneal the metal, and continue forming the band until you have a circular ring. Anneal the ring again.

3. Bring the ends of the ring together and file flush. (The ring does not have to be completely round at this point. The two ends only need to meet and be flush.) Solder the ends together with hard solder; pickle, rinse, and dry the ring. Remove any excess solder with a file, then sand the ring with 320- and 400-grit sandpaper.

4. Place the ring on a mandrel, and use your hands to twist the ring down to bring it back to a round shape. Tap the inside of the U-shape with the narrow end of the nylon hammer. If you need to enlarge the ring, tap the inside of the U-shape with an embossing hammer to stretch it.

5. To make the edges level, place the ring on a flat steel block, and hammer gently with the flat face of a planishing hammer. Repeat this step on the opposite side of the ring. Take care to be gentle—too much pressure will collapse the ring.

6. Place the ring on the mandrel and tap the edges with a narrow-faced hammer to give them texture. Sand the inside and outside surfaces of the ring with 400-grit sandpaper, then use a brass brush.

7. Add colored rubber bands to the U-shape by twisting them around the ring and layering them as desired.

▶ ▶ Get Set

Sterling silver round wire,
14 gauge, 3 inches
(7.6 cm)

Sterling silver round wire,
20 gauge, ¾ inch
(1.9 cm)

Sterling silver charm with
hole, 7 mm

Bench tool kit, page 9

Soldering kit, page 9

Letter stamps

Liver of sulfur

FINISHED SIZE
2 x 2.5 cm

DESIGNER'S NOTE
Instead of stamping a tag,
you can use a pre-made
charm or a bead to hang
from the cat shape.

▶ ▶ ▶ Go

1. Determine and cut the proper length of
14-gauge sterling silver wire for your desired
ring size. File the wire ends flat.

2. Form the wire around a ring mandrel with
a rawhide mallet to make a circle. Solder
the ends of the circle together. Pickle, rinse,
and dry the metal. Place the circle on a ring
mandrel and hammer with a mallet to make
the ring fully round. File and sand the
solder joint.

3. Cut two 1-inch (2.5 cm) lengths of
14-gauge sterling silver wire. File the wire
ends flat.

4. Mark the center of each wire. Make a
V-shaped notch in the center of each wire
with a square file. File this notch three
quarters of the way through the wire.

5. Use chain-nose pliers to shape the wires
into ear shapes. Snip each wire "ear" to the
desired size, and file the ends so they fit
snug next to the ring.

6. Position the ring and wire "ears" flat on
a soldering block. Solder all the joints and
solder the V-shaped notches. Pickle, rinse,
and dry the ring.

7. Using a letter stamp, a chasing hammer,
and a steel block, stamp the charm. Make
a 4-mm jump ring from the 20-gauge wire.
Use the jump ring to attach the charm to
the ring shank. Solder the jump ring closed.
Pickle, rinse, and dry the ring. File and sand
the joint.

8. Use a liver-of-sulfur solution to give the
ring a patina. Brush the ring with steel wool.

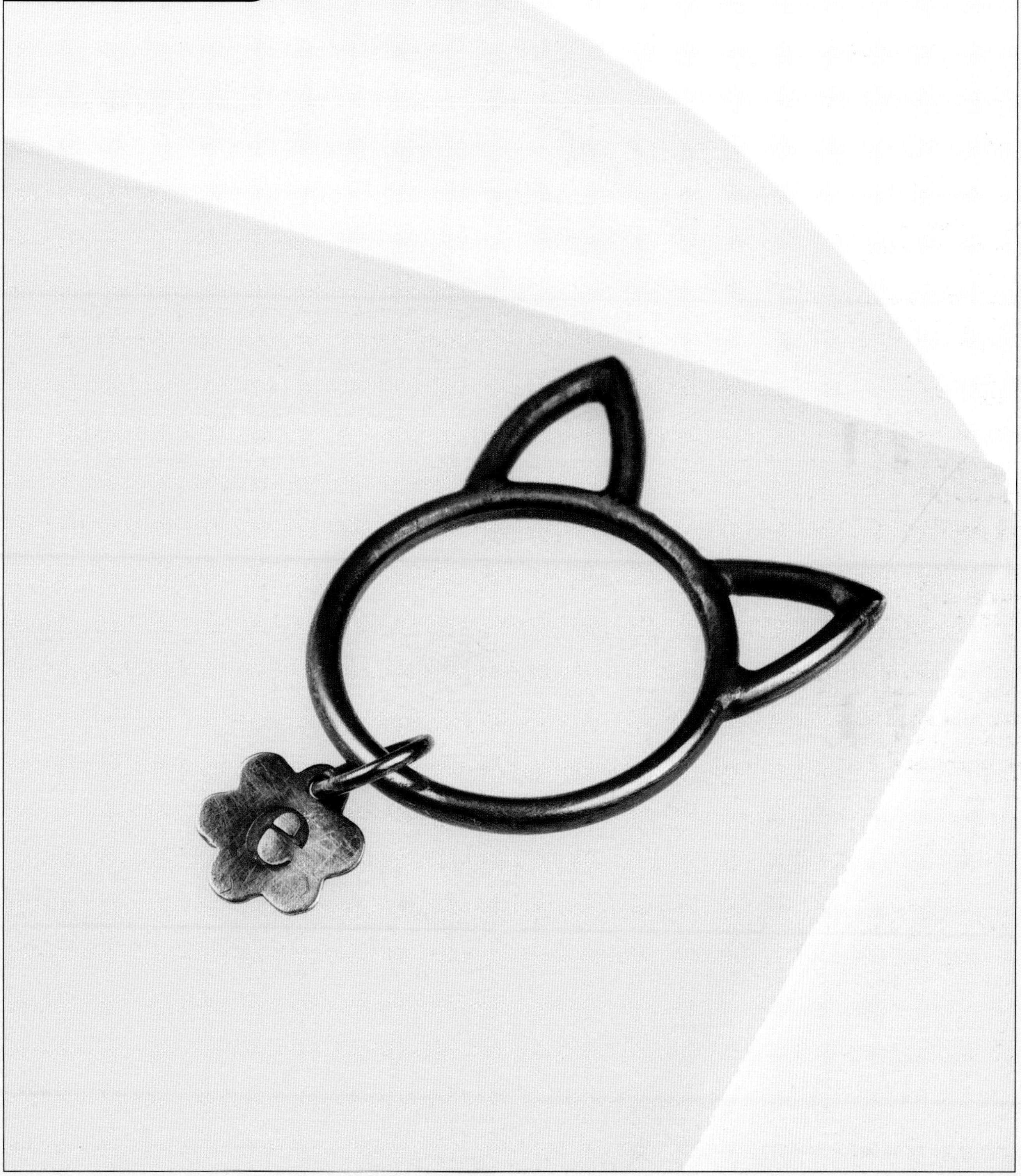

SAWING • FILING • SANDBLASTING • SOLDERING • POLISHING USING TWO-PART EPOXY

► ► **Get Set**

Sterling silver sheet,
12 gauge, 2 x 1¼ inches
(5 x 3 cm)

Sterling silver wire,
20 gauge, ¼ inch
(6 mm)

Onyx tear drop, half drilled

Photocopied design
template ❶

Bench tool kit, page 9

Soldering kit, page 9

FINISHED SIZE
4.3 x 2.2 x 0.5 cm

► ► ► **Go**

1. Using the photocopied design template, transfer the ring design onto the 12-gauge sterling silver sheet.

2. Pierce and saw out the finger hole, then saw the outside shape of the design.

3. File and sand all cut metal edges.

4. Solder the 20-gauge wire to the center of the top of the ring band. Pickle, rinse, and dry the metal.

5. Finish the surface of the ring with a brass brush.

6. Use two-part epoxy to adhere the onyx teardrop to the 20-gauge wire, making sure the stone sits flush with the ring band.

❶

FILING • SAWING • FORMING • SOLDERING • SANDING POLISHING • PEG SETTING

Get Set

Sterling silver flat wire, 3 x 1.2 x 75 mm

Sterling silver round wire, 20 gauge, 5 mm

Pink pearl, half drilled, 5 mm

Epoxy

Bench tool kit, page 9

Soldering kit, page 9

Narrow cord

FINISHED SIZE 2 x 2 x 3 cm

Go

1. File the edges of the silver flat wire smooth. Wrap the wire around a ring mandrel so the middle bends but the ends remain straight, creating a teardrop shape.

2. Slide the flat wire down the mandrel to the desired ring size. Saw the excess wire off the ends. Solder the top of the ring closed, keeping the teardrop shape. File the soldered joint.

3. Hold the pink pearl inside the peak of the ring so that the edges of the pearl touch each side. Use a scribe to mark the inside of the ring at the pearl's hole location.

4. File the end of the 20-gauge wire. Hold the wire with cross-locking tweezers. Ball a solder snippet on the end of the wire. Solder the wire into place at the mark on the inside of the ring. Pickle, rinse, and dry the metal.

5. Snip the wire peg to fit inside the pearl.

6. File and sand the ring inside and out. Polish the metal to a rouge shine. To polish inside the peak of the teardrop, tie the cord to the bench and rub with polishing compound. Hold the cord taut, and slide the ring up and down the cord.

7. Clean off all buffing compound. Place a small drop of epoxy on the peg, and slide the pearl in place. Let the epoxy dry.

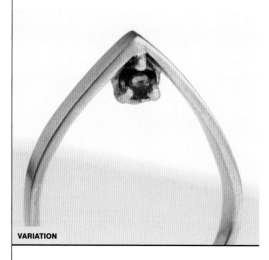

VARIATION

→▶ ▶ **Get Set**

Brass tubing, 1¼ inches
(3.2 cm) OD

Sterling silver rectangular
wire, 5 x 1.5 mm,
1½ inches (3.8 cm)

Bench tool kit, page 9

Soldering tool kit, page 9

Ring gauge set

Belt sander, optional

FINISHED SIZE
3.2 x 3.2 x 0.5 cm

DESIGNER'S NOTE
A metal lathe will cut the
tubing much faster than a
jeweler's saw or a
pipe cutter.

▶ ▶ ▶ **Go**

1. Using a pipe cutter or a jeweler's saw,
cut a 5-mm length of brass tubing. Sand
the cut edges of the tubing smooth.
Sand the inside of the ring with emery paper
in a slotted mandrel on a flexible shaft.

2. Select the desired size from a ring gauge
set. Measure the interior diameter of the
desired size.

3. Form the sterling silver rectangular wire
into a soft curve by bending the wire around
a ring or bracelet mandrel and tapping it
with a rawhide mallet.

4. Saw the curved silver wire to the length
needed so the negative space of the ring will
accommodate your finger size. File the ends
of the silver wire to the correct angle to fit
inside the brass tubing.

5. Solder the curved silver wire inside the
brass tubing. Pickle, rinse, and dry the ring.

6. Sand the ring flush on a flat piece of
sandpaper or a belt sander.

7. To put a consistent finish on the ring,
sand the inside and outside of the ring
with emery paper in a slotted mandrel on a
flexible shaft.

Want To Make Another Ring?

As shown in the project photo, there are
many variations on this simple design. Use
three small curved wires instead of one larger
one, or solder silver tubing to the interior of
the brass tube.

▶ ▶ **Get Set**

Half-drilled pearl

Sterling silver round wire, gauge corresponding to the hole in the pearl

Sterling silver casting grain or scrap silver for casting

Bench tool kit, page 9

Soldering kit, page 9

Two-part epoxy

Crucible for melting metal

Borax powder

Cuttlefish

Toothbrush

FINISHED SIZE
2.4 x 2.4 x 0.6 cm

DESIGNER'S NOTE
If you end up with flashing from your cuttlefish pour, either cut it off or keep it as part of your design.

▶ ▶ ▶ **Go**

1. Prepare the cuttlefish by cutting it in half, then rubbing the halves together in a circular motion to flatten out both sides for the largest working area.

2. Widen the top of each side of the cuttlefish with a spoon to form the funnel. Using a triangular needle file, carve a long, thin, flat line at least 1 mm deep and a minimum of 15 mm from the bottom of the cuttlefish. Note: The longer the area you carve, the more ring size options you will have.

3. Use a toothbrush to clean the dust from the depressions on each side of the cuttlefish. Secure the two sides of the cuttlefish together with masking tape. Place the cuttlefish securely upright in the soldering area.

4. Melt the silver casting grain with a pinch of borax in a crucible, using a little more silver than you think you need. (The extra metal will form the casting button in the funnel.) When the silver is completely molten, slowly pour the metal into the funnel in the cuttlefish. Let the metal cool and open the cuttlefish. Remove the metal with tweezers and quench it in water.

5. Clean the metal with a matte wheel on a buffing machine or a flexible shaft. Cut off the button with a saw.

6. Using a plastic hammer, form the cast metal piece around a ring mandrel to the desired ring size. Cut any extra length, allowing plenty of room for the pearl.

7. Curve the button end with a round file so the pearl fits nicely. Solder a 1-inch (2.5 cm) piece of sterling silver wire to the middle of the carved end. Snip the wire to a length that allows the pearl to sit snugly next to the cast ring.

8. Buff the ring with a matte wheel on a polishing machine or flexible shaft to brighten the silver without losing its texture. Rub the inside of the ring with steel wool.

9. Glue the pearl in place using two-part epoxy, and let dry.

Want to Make Another Ring?

If you have old gold jewelry you no longer wear, you can melt it down to make this project. Using a different color pearl is another option.

▶▶ ▶ Get Set

Sterling silver flat wire,
  2 x 8 mm, 2½ inches
  (6.4 cm)

Sterling silver round wire,
  18 gauge, 1 inch
  (2.5 cm)

Rough stone, 6 to 10 mm

Bench tool kit, page 9

Soldering kit, page 9

Fine pumice wheel

FINISHED SIZE
2.5 x 2 x 0.8 cm

▶ ▶ ▶ Go

1. Determine the length of the sterling silver flat wire needed for your desired ring size. Mark and cut the metal at this point. File the ends of the wire flat, and solder them together.

2. Place the wire ring on a ring mandrel and hammer it with a rawhide mallet. File and sand the ring to a 400-grit finish.

3. Place the stone on the top of the ring, opposite the solder joint. Using a permanent marker, mark the metal at four equidistant points around the stone. (These indicate where you will place the prongs.) Indent each marked point with a scribe.

4. Using a 1-mm bit, drill a 1-mm-deep hole at each indention on the ring. Do not drill through the band.

5. Use snips to cut the 18-gauge round wire into four sections. Solder one length of 18-gauge wire into each hole. Give the ring a final finish by brushing it with a brass brush or rubbing it with steel wool.

6. Place the stone in the prongs. Use chain-nose pliers to bend the prongs securely over the stone. Snip any extra wire. Use flat-nose pliers to wiggle each prong side to side, creating a tight hold with each prong on the stone.

7. Give the end of each prong a smooth finish by using a fine pumice wheel in a flexible shaft.

▶▶ Get Set

Sterling silver rectangle wire, 3 x 1 mm, 4 inches (10.2 cm)

Bench tool kit, page 9

Soldering kit, page 9

FINISHED SIZE
2 x 2 x 1.5 cm

DESIGNER'S NOTE
This ring is designed to have a small gap between the leaf and bud and is adjustable. The instructions are given for a size 6½ ring.

▶▶▶ Go

1. Measure and cut two pieces of rectangular wire for the leaf form, each ⅝ inch (1.6 cm) long. Measure and cut one 2.5-cm piece of rectangular wire for the bud and one 4-cm piece for the shank. File the ends of the cut wire flat.

2. Use half-round pliers to bend the 2.5-cm wire length into a round shape, making sure the ends meet flush. Solder the wire joint. Pickle, rinse, and dry the wire circle. Tap the circle with a rawhide mallet on a ring mandrel to adjust the shape.

3. At the size-4 mark on a ring mandrel, bend each 1.6-cm wire length to form an arc. Sand the wire ends by rubbing each arc on a flat sheet of 220-grit sandpaper. Solder the arcs together, making sure the joints are flush.

4. File the ends of the shank wire with a half round file to match the curves on the sides of the bud and leaf. Flatten the wire on a steel block with a rawhide mallet.

5. Place the shank wire on a flat soldering block, and position the leaf and bud at the corresponding filed ends, making sure there are no gaps. Solder the joints. Pickle, rinse, and dry the ring.

6. Soften the wire edges, and remove any solder marks with a file. Sand all surfaces to a 400-grit finish.

7. Bend the ring around the ring mandrel. Tap it with a rawhide mallet to shape and work-harden the metal until it is the desired shape and size. Finish the ring by rubbing it with steel wool.

Want To Make Another Ring?

Alter the leaf and bud shapes, and use round wire instead of flat wire. Replace one shape with a tube-set faceted stone or a cabochon.

DESIGNER: **CAROLE ZAKKOUR**

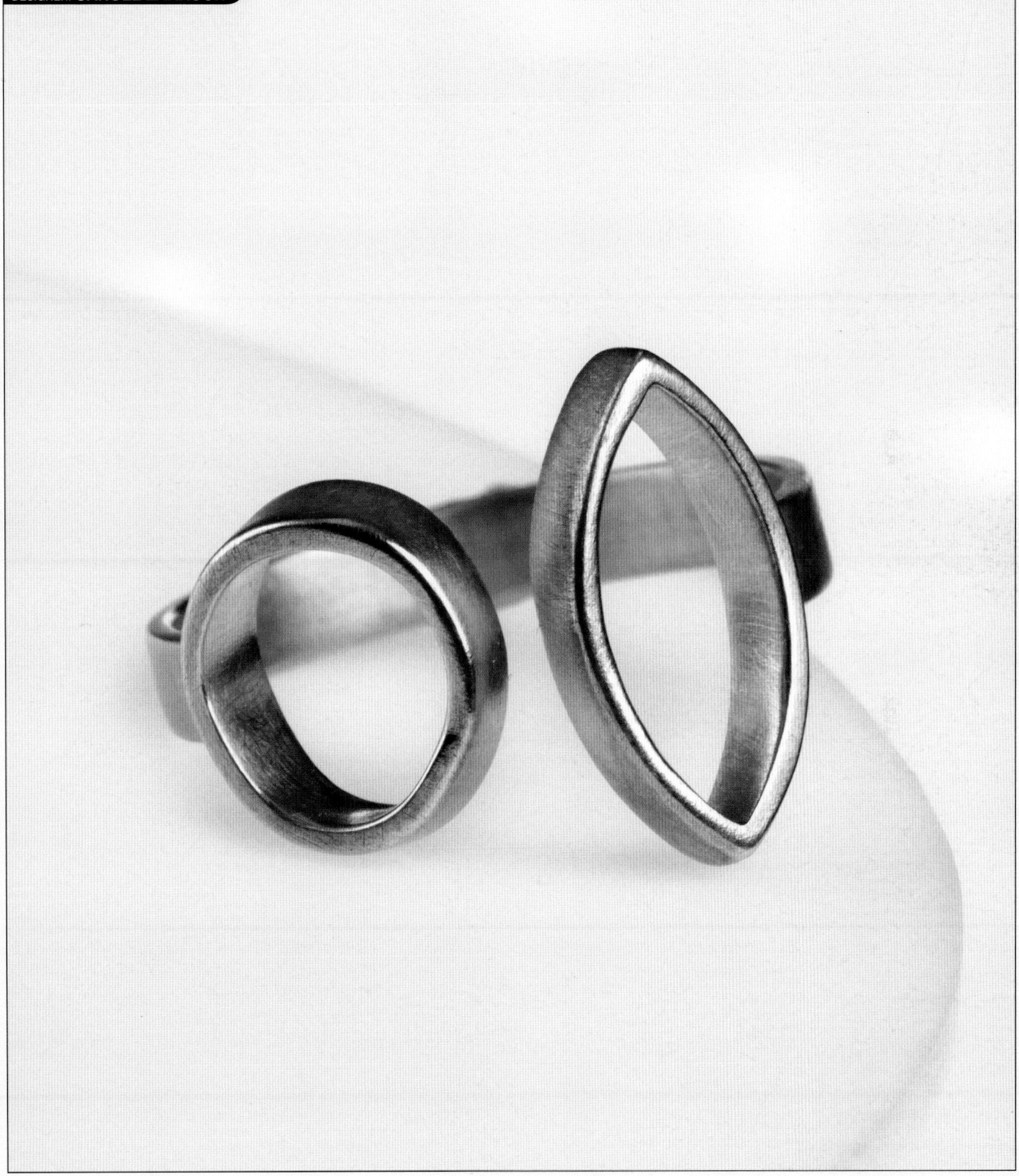

DESIGNER: **SHIRLEE GRUND**

→► **Get Set**

Sterling silver half-round wire, 12 gauge, 5 inches (12.7 cm)

Bench tool kit, page 9

Soldering tool kit, page 9

FINISHED SIZE
Band, ½ inch (1.3 cm) wide

DESIGNER'S NOTE
Two concentric rings of half-round wire cross to form an X-shape. The interior ring has the flat side out, and the outer ring is formed with the flat side in, making them quick and easy to solder together.

►►► **Go**

1. Determine your ring size. Add one quarter to one half of a size to that measurement. (Because this ring crosses your finger at an angle instead of straight across, you need to make it a bit larger than your actual size.) With flush cutting wire snips, cut one piece of 12-gauge half-round wire to this length.

2. Bend the cut wire into a band with the flat side facing out. True the ends with a file, and bring them flush together. Solder the seam. Pickle, rinse, and dry the silver band.

3. Place the silver band on a ring mandrel, and form it into a perfect circle with a mallet.

4. Determine the measurement for a ring that is one size larger than the one cut in step 1. Cut the 12-gauge half-round wire to this length. Bend the wire into a band with the round side facing out. True the ends with a file, and bring them flush together. Solder the seam. Pickle, rinse, and dry the silver band.

5. Check the bands for fit. One needs to fit snugly inside the other. If necessary, stretch one of the bands on the ring mandrel with a mallet.

6. Cross the two bands to form an X-shape. Adjust the angle to make sure you'll be able to comfortably slide your finger through the ring. Hold the ring in cross-locking tweezers, then flux and solder both joints. Pickle, rinse, brass brush, and dry the ring.

7. Because the two circles cross at an angle, the opening of the ring is now ovoid. Slide the ring onto the mandrel, and bring it back into round. Do not hammer.

Want To Make Another Ring?

Embellish this elegant ring by adding a tube-set stone to one of the intersections of the X-shaped wires.

⟶▶ **Get Set**

Sterling silver round wire, 14 gauge, 7 inches (17.8 cm)

Sterling silver bezel to fit stone

Stone of your choice to fit bezel

Bench tool kit, page 9

Soldering kit, page 9

FINISHED SIZE
2.5 x 2.5 x 0.7 cm

DESIGNER'S NOTE
For a larger or smaller ring, adjust the length of the wires accordingly.

▶ ▶ ▶ **Go**

1. Cut six pieces of 14-gauge silver wire, each 1.8 cm long.

2. Position three of the wires in a semicircle, stacking their ends so one end is on top and one end is under the adjacent wires. Add three more wire lengths for a total of six wires. You will notice a circle is forming. Solder the wires at each joint, leaving the last joint open.

3. Place the ring on a ring mandrel, and open or close it to the proper size. Solder the last joint closed, making sure the end of the last wire is underneath the first wire length to maintain the pattern. Pickle, rinse, and dry the ring.

4. Shape the ring on the mandrel again, gently tapping it with a rawhide mallet until it is the correct size.

5. Repeat steps 1 through 4 to create a second ring.

6. Stack the two rings, and solder them together at each joint. Trim the excess length from each wire, and use a file, a cup burr, or sandpaper to round the ends. Determine which side you want to be the top of the ring, and solder the bezel in the center of that wire section. Pickle, rinse, and dry the ring.

7. Tumble the ring to polish the metal, and set the stone in the bezel.

Have Time To Spare?

Use square wire and channel set the stones, or make a stack of three or four of the bands to create a really wide ring.

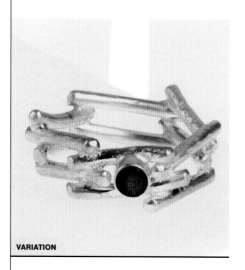

VARIATION

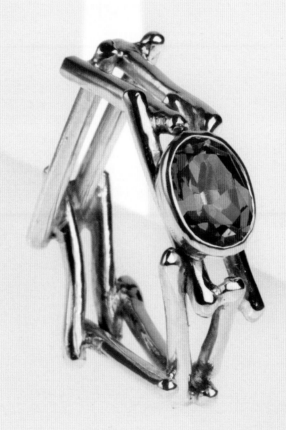

SAWING • FILING • FORMING • SOLDERING • SANDING • FINISHING

→▶ **Get Set**

**Sterling silver round wire,
16 gauge, 12 inches
(30.5 cm)**

**Sterling silver square wire,
16 gauge, 6 inches
(15.2 cm)**

Bench tool kit, page 9

Soldering kit, page 9

**FINISHED SIZE
5 x 3.2 cm**

→▶▶ **Go**

1. Cut two pieces of the 16-gauge round wire to the proper length for your desired ring size. File the ends of each wire flat.

2. Using a hammer and a ring mandrel, form each wire into the shape of a ring until the ends meet perfectly. Solder the joints. Pickle and rinse the rings.

3. Hammer each ring round on a ring mandrel. File and sand the solder joints.

4. Cut eight pieces of the 16-gauge square wire, each ½ inch (1.3 cm) long. Form each of the wires into identical arcs with half-round pliers.

5. Hammer the arcs smooth on a small anvil. File the ends of the wires so the arcs sit upright on a flat surface.

6. Using cross-locking tweezers and a pair of third hands, set up the two rings and one arc for soldering. Solder the two joints. Use a third hand to hold the next wire arc in place on the opposite side of the ring. Solder the two joints. Continue in this manner until all eight arcs are soldered in place. Pickle, rinse, and dry the ring.

7. File and sand all solder joints. Polish and finish the ring as desired.

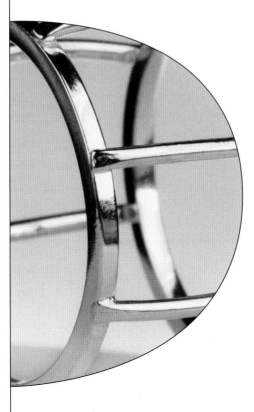

▶▶ ▶ Get Set

Sterling silver sheet,
  18 gauge,
  1¼ x 1¼ inches
  (3.2 x 3.2 cm)

Sterling silver round wire,
  12 gauge, 2¾ inches
  (7 cm)

Photocopied design
  template ❶

Bench tool kit, page 9

Soldering kit, page 9

FINISHED SIZE
Top element, 3.2 x 3.2 cm

▶▶ ▶ Go

1. Saw out the sterling silver shape using the photocopied template as a guide. File the edges of the silver shape. Using a circular motion, sand its front and back surfaces with 220-grit sandpaper.

2. Following the design on the template, use a scribe and a ruler to draw lines on the silver, connecting the points where the scallops meet.

3. Use snips to cut the 12-gauge sterling silver round wire to the proper length for the desired ring size. File the ends of the wire, and remove all burrs. Bend the wire with half round pliers and your fingers to connect the ends. Flux and solder the ring closed with hard solder. Pickle, rinse, and dry the ring.

4. File and sand the ring's solder joint if needed. Place the ring on a ring mandrel, and hammer it round.

5. Place the scalloped silver piece on a piece of soft wood. Use a center punch and utility hammer to indent dots along the scribed lines, each approximately 1 to 2 mm apart, beginning at points where the lines cross or end.

6. File a flat spot on the ring shank at its solder seam. Flux the ring at the flat spot, and melt a small piece of medium solder at that spot.

7. Flux the back of the scalloped piece and place it face down on soldering block. Use a third hand and cross-locking tweezers to hold the ring in place, centered on the scalloped top. Solder the ring together by re-melting the medium solder you put on the flat spot in step 6. Pickle, rinse, and dry the ring. Finish it with a brass brush.

Want to Make Another Ring?

Scribe any pattern on your scalloped sheet, and punch along those lines.

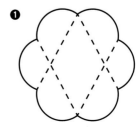

❶

→ Get Ready

USING A ROLLING MILL • **ANNEALING** • **SOLDERING** • **DRILLING** **ADDING A PATINA** • **FINISHING**

→ ▶ **Get Set**

Sterling silver round
wire, 12 to 18 gauge,
minimum 20 inches
(50.8 cm)

Sterling silver round
wire, 22 or 24 gauge
(depending on the size
of the bead hole),
2 inches (5.1 cm)

Bench tool kit, page 9

Soldering kit, page 9

Liver of sulfur

FINISHED SIZE
Variable, based on size of
ring and height of bead

DESIGNER'S NOTE
You can use rectangular
wire for this project instead
of rolling down round wire,
but the edges will be
more rigid.

▶ ▶ ▶ **Go**

1. Roll the 12- to 18-gauge round wire through the rolling mill until it measures between 18 and 22 gauge, depending on your preference.

2. Anneal the wire. Leaving 1 inch (2.5 cm) of wire sticking out, wrap the flattened wire around a ring mandrel several times at the mark indicating the desired ring size. Overlap the wire to make the ring thick or thin, wide or slender.

3. Remove the wrapped ring from the mandrel, making sure the coils stay together. Each end of the wire should be sticking up about 1 inch (2.5 cm), and about ½ inch (1.3 cm) apart for the bead.

4. Using three or four pieces of binding wire, firmly wrap the wires of the ring together. Solder the wires together at several different points of contact for stability.

5. Place the bead between the wires that are sticking up. Snip each wire end slightly above the bead hole. If the wire is thin, ball up the ends of the wires, hammer them flat, and drill a hole in each. If the wire is thick, round the edges with a file and then drill the holes. The drill hole should be slightly larger than the diameter of the wire you use to secure the bed.

6. Ball one end of the 22- or 24-gauge wire. Insert this wire through one hole in the ring wire, through the bead, and through the opposite hole in the ring wire. Snip the bead wire, leaving 4 mm sticking out.

7. With a very hot flame, ball up the remaining end of the wire to secure the bead in place. The flame should be hot enough that it will quickly melt the metal and not burn the bead. You do not need to pickle after this step since the ring will be blackened.

8. Immerse the ring into a patina solution until it becomes black. Rub the ring with steel wool or sandpaper for a final finish.

Want to Make Another Ring?

To create a different style, give the wire a hammered texture or roller print it before wrapping it around the mandrel.

►► ► Get Set

Sterling silver round wire,
10 gauge, ¹³⁄₁₆ inch
(2.1 cm), annealed

Sterling silver round wire,
12 gauge, 2¼ inches
(5.7 cm)

2 sterling silver round
wires, 12 gauge, each
1½ inches (3.8 cm) long

2 sterling silver round
wires, 12 gauge, each
¹⁵⁄₁₆ inch (1 cm) long

Bench tool kit, page 9

Soldering kit, page 9

FINISHED SIZE
6.4 x 3.1 x 5 cm

►►► Go

1. Using a plastic mallet, hammer the annealed 10-gauge silver wire around a ring mandrel until the ends are approximately 2.5 mm apart.

2. Anneal all five lengths of the 12-gauge silver wire. With a flat metal hammer, tap one end of each 12-gauge wire, reducing the thickness to 1 mm. Set the rollers on the rolling mill 1 mm apart. With the flattened end forward, run each wire through the rolling mill. Anneal the silver wires. Reset the rollers on the rolling mill 0.5 mm apart. Run the wires through the rolling mill once more.

3. Round off one end of each flattened wire with a file. Remove any sharp burrs and corners with sandpaper, then sand the full length of each flattened wire.

4. On a soldering block, arrange the flattened silver wires in the 2.5-mm space between the ends of the band. Place the shortest wires on the outside of the group and the longest wires in the center. Solder each wire to the adjacent wire and to the ends of the band.

5. With a rawhide mallet, tap the edges of the flattened wires to work-harden them. Rub the ring with a green scrub pad to create the final matte finish.

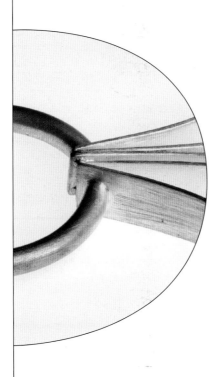

TEXTURING · SAWING · FILING · ANNEALING · FORMING SOLDERING · TAPERING · FINISHING

▶ Get Set

Sterling silver sheet,
20 gauge, 3 inches
(7.6 cm) square

Sterling silver wire,
6 gauge, 2¾ inches
(7 cm)

Photocopied design
template ❶

Bench tool kit, page 9

Soldering kit, page 9

FINISHED SIZE
7.6 x 1.9 x 3.2 cm

DESIGNER'S NOTE
The top wave can be textured using hammers, roller printing, or acid etching.

▶ ▶ ▶ Go

1. Texture the silver sheet with a goldsmith's hammer, horizontally to the grain.

2. Trace the photocopied template onto the silver sheet. Cut out the traced shapes with a jeweler's saw. File the cut metal edges. Pierce and saw the interior lines on each silver shape according to the template.

3. Anneal both silver shapes, and let them air cool. Do not quench.

4. Form the shapes with plastic-coated pliers so the "waves" undulate. Link the forms as desired. Solder the silver forms together at the points where they meet.

5. Cut the 6-gauge sterling silver wire to the proper length for the desired ring size. Anneal the wire.

6. Taper both ends of the 6-gauge wire with a planishing hammer, and file the ends smooth. Re-anneal the wire.

7. With a plastic hammer, form the 6-gauge wire around a ring mandrel, keeping the ends open ¼ inch (6 mm).

8. Solder the finished silver form to the ring shank. Pickle, rinse, and dry the metal.

9. Finish the ring with a satin wheel, and burnish the metal for highlights where desired.

❶

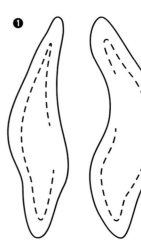

⮞⮞ ⮞ **Get Set**

2 sterling silver disks,
22 gauge, each
1¾ inches (4.5 cm)

Bench tool kit, page 9

Soldering kit, page 9

FINISHED SIZE
3.5 x 3.5 x 1.5 cm

DESIGNER'S NOTE
If you wish to wear this ring on the ring or middle finger, you may want to cut or file space from the domes to accommodate the neighboring fingers.

⮞⮞ ⮞ **Go**

1. Using a large dapping block and punch, slightly dap both 22-gauge silver disks to the same depth.

2. Determine where you want the randomly spaced drill holes and the finger opening. Mark these locations on the domed disks. Gently center punch each drill-hole location. Using bit sizes of your choice, drill the holes.

3. Pierce and saw out one finger hole in each domed disk, making sure the holes are the same size and fit the finger comfortably.

4. Use a large coarse file to file the edges of the disks flat. Place the disks on sandpaper resting on a flat surface, and sand the disk edges flat.

5. Solder the domed disks together, making sure the circumferences match and the solder joint is tight. Pickle, rinse, and dry the ring.

6. File or sand the inside of the ring holes for a comfortable fit. Sand the outside of the ring with 320-grit sandpaper.

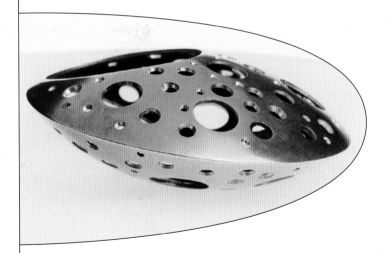

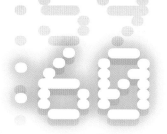

SCORING • ANNEALING • USING A ROLLING MILL • SOLDERING FILING • SANDING • FORMING • USING A DISK CUTTER • DOMING ADDING A PATINA • PEG SETTING

▶▶▶ Get Set

Bimetal sheet, 18 karat, 20 gauge, 5½ x ⅜ inch (14 x 1 cm)

Sterling silver sheet, 16 gauge, 5½ x ⅜ inch (14 x 1 cm)

Sterling silver round wire, 18 gauge, 1 inch (2.5 cm)

Round black pearl, half drilled, 7 mm

Bench tool kit, page 9

Soldering kit, page 9

French curve

Two-part epoxy

FINISHED SIZE
2.8 x 2.2 x 2.5 cm

DESIGNER'S NOTE
Instead of drawing diagonal lines on the bimetal sheet, you can draw straight lines or use a ball burr to cut small dots.

▶▶▶ Go

1. Use a black marker to draw a pattern of diagonal stripes on the bimetal sheet. Using a flexible shaft with a cutting wheel, score the pattern on the bimetal until the silver is exposed, making sure not to cut too deep.

2. Anneal the bimetal sheet, and place it between two sheets of paper. Roll the stack through the rolling mill.

3. Sweat solder the bimetal sheet onto the sheet of 16-gauge sterling silver. Pickle, rinse, and dry the metal. Saw or file the ends flush.

4. Using calipers, measure and mark one end of the sheet 9 mm wide. Measure and mark the other end 7 mm in from the edge.

5. Line up the marks with a French curve ruler, and scribe a curved line onto the metal along the ruler's edge. Saw off the metal along the marked curve. File the edges and sand them to a 400-grit finish.

6. Using a plastic mallet, round the metal strip on a ring mandrel. Smooth the edges of the ring shank with a flexible shaft and sanding wheel.

7. Use a disk cutter to punch a 10-mm disk from the silver sheet. Dome the disk with a dapping block and punch.

8. Solder the silver dome onto the ring shank with the concave side facing up. Solder the 18-gauge round wire to the center of the concave side of the dome. Pickle, rinse, and dry the ring.

9. Use liver of sulfur to patina the ring. Brass brush it, and burnish its edges.

10. Trim the peg to the appropriate length for the pearl, and secure the pearl to the peg with epoxy.

CONTRIBUTING DESIGNERS

2 Roses Studio makes odd things from even odder materials from their Southern California studio. Their equally odd website can be seen at www.2roses.com.

Melinda Alexander has been teaching jewelry making for almost four years, and she loves it as much as making jewelry. For her, the creation of each piece is a wonderful experience, and she hopes that one day her kids will find the sanity in her new creations and ideas.

Eleni Avloniti is a jewelry designer from Corfu, Greece, who strives to create works of art that show the marriage between simplicity and form. Most of her inspiration for jewelry comes from traveling and from her Mediterranean surroundings. For further information, visit www.mod3rnart.com and www.mod3rnart.etsy.com.

Ruth Avra draws inspiration from nature and combines traditional metal-working techniques with exotic materials such as stingray, and she even uses her sister's oil-on-canvas paintings as the backdrop for her unique designs. Every piece of jewelry and its components are always handmade by Ruth herself, allowing for the utmost quality and attention to detail. Ruth's work can be found in boutiques and galleries around the world and at www.ruthavra.com.

Emma Baird is a metal clay and lampwork artist based in Edinburgh. She established Scotland's first metal clay training studio and continues to run a wide variety of metal clay courses for Art Clay Scotland.

Boris Bally's award-winning work is both witty and innovative. His current repertoire transforms recycled street signs, weapon parts, and other found materials into objects for the home and body. Boris has received several prestigious fellowships, and his work is featured in numerous international exhibitions and publications.

Colleen Baran is a Canadian jewelry designer who has exhibited and been published in more than 10 countries. Recent publications include the Lark Crafts books *500 Wedding Rings* (2008) and *500 Plastic Jewelry Designs* (2009). Additionally, she has won local and international awards for jewelry and photography.

Raïssa Bump teaches and makes jewelry and knitwear. She is thrilled to contribute her own designs to the rich history of adornment. Her work can be seen at www.raissabump.com.

Juan Carlos Caballero-Perez is a metal artist and educator who came to the United States in 1986 from Mexico City, Mexico. Carlos works as an associate professor in the metals program at Rochester Institute of Technology, where he started in 2001 following the receipt of bachelor's and master's degrees from the same institute. A New York State Foundation of the Arts Fellowship Recipient and Craft Alliance of New York State Career Development Grant recipient, Carlos creates jewelry and large public sculptures out of his studio in Rochester, NY.

Katarina Cudic was born in 1978 in Serbia. Through jewelry making, she explores and tries to reconcile and combine the past, present, and future. Recently, Katarina has found inspiration in nature, especially in wood, and uses different species of wood to achieve forms or texture found in nature. Katarina studied at the jewelry school *Le Arti Orafe* in Florence and has earned a degree from the department of art history, Faculty of Philosophy, in Belgrade. Her website is www.katarinacudic.com.

Cynthia Del Giudice is an Argentine-American metalsmith based in the Argentine Pampas. She uses a variety of metals and recycled or sustainable materials for her creations. Her work can be found at www.cynthiadelgiudice.etsy.com and www.cynthiadelgiudice.blogspot.com.

Molly Dingledine is a studio jeweler working in Asheville, NC. She graduated in 2005 from the Savannah College of Art and Design with a BFA in Metals and Jewelry. She is represented in galleries throughout the country and sells her work at fine craft shows. Fascinated with its forms and textures, the natural world has always been Molly's source of inspiration, whether it's found on mountain trails or city streets. She builds on the simple shapes found in nature to create complex art forms. Her work can be seen at www.mollydingledine.com.

Nina Dinoff creates jewelry that focuses on the interplay of simple geometric form with the complex, organic nature of the body. Her work is influenced by her background in graphic design and by her love of Modernism. She lives and works in Brooklyn, NY. You can see her work at www.ninadinoffjewelry.com.

Robert Dudenhoefer II is a graduate of the University of Michigan with a BFA in Metalwork & Jewelry Design. He currently resides in Corvallis, OR, where he creates an original line of sterling silver jewelry, as well as larger sculptural pieces from reclaimed materials. He is continually adding new techniques and materials to his designs in order to fabricate detailed pieces that are unique, articulated, and whimsical. Robert's work can be found at www.robdudedesigns.com.

Aja Engel attended the University of Nebraska-Lincoln where she studied printmaking and painting. She currently resides in Chicago, IL, where she continues to explore metal etching, texture, and color at the Lill Street Art Center metalsmithing studio. You can find her work www.ajaengel.com.

Dilyana Evtimova lives and works in West Midlands, United Kingdom. She graduated in 2007 from the University of Wolverhampton in three-dimensional contemporary applied arts. She was selected as a jeweler in residence in Bilston Craft Gallery, designing and making jewelry for retail and private commissions. She strives to capture the beauty and fragility of organic forms. You can find her work at www.dilyana.co.uk.

Shelby Ferris Fitzpatrick is continually exploring new materials and concepts for jewelry as a catalyst for social interaction through her project-based work. New dimensions are found in her work through the integration of the five senses, light, or movement. Her use of interchangeable parts in her designs are a constant source of new choices for the wearer. Shelby's work can be found at www.shelbyfitzpatrick.com.

Brittany Golden is the resident artist and silversmith instructor at the Sundance Resort in Utah. She creates jewelry and teaches classes from her personal studio in Provo. Her work is on display in the Sundance Gallery and at www.brittanygolden.com and www.brittanygoldenstudio.com.

Joanna Gollberg is a studio jeweler in Asheville, NC. In addition to making jewelry, she is the author of four Lark Crafts books: *Making Metal Jewelry* (2006), *Creative Metal Crafts* (2005), *The Art and Craft of Making Jewelry* (2006), and *The Ultimate Jeweler's Guide* (2010). Joanna teaches jewelry making at craft schools, such as The Penland School of Craft and Arrowmont Craft School, as well as for metalsmithing groups across the country. She exhibits her work at fine craft shows and galleries nationally.

Shirlee Grund makes handcrafted jewelry with clean lines and dirty textures. Her work has been exhibited across the country, landing descriptions such as "beautiful and not the least bit frilly" and "infinitely satisfying." Shirlee earned her BFA from Tufts University and the School of the Museum of Fine Arts in Boston, MA. She now takes commissions as a studio jeweler in Seattle, WA, working under the name Lichen & Lychee. To learn more about Shirlee, visit www.lichenandlychee.com.

Rebecca Hannon has her own workshop and teaches full time at the Nova Scotia College of Art & Design in Canada. "I work in series. In each new grouping there is a challenge to create tension between the story and the right medium to evoke meaning. Materials are endless; one must search and then concentrate to find the subtle message found in an object."

Denise Harrison stumbled upon a metals program three years ago that transformed her life for the better. She has discovered a creative, yet technical process that allows her to take what she sees in her surroundings to create truly gratifying interpretations of that vision. You can find more of her work at www.pikapika-design.com.

Lora Hart first started exploring metal clay and traditional jewelry fabrication techniques at the turn of the century. Fully committed to the art, she now creates silver jewels in her charming Venice Beach studio and teaches metal clay throughout the greater Los Angeles area. See Lora's work at www.lorahart.com.

Catherine Hodge is a jewelry designer, former teacher, and a stay-at-home mom to two little boys. She creates jewelry with a focus on texture, feminine elements, and little touches of whimsy. See more of her work at www.catherinemarissa.com or www.catherinemarissa.etsy.com.

Nicole Jacquard lives and works in Bloomington, IN, where she maintains her studio and teaches at Indiana University. More of her work can be found at www.nicolejacquard.com.

Mariann Monika Kiss completed an Advanced Diploma in Jewelry Engineering Technology in Melbourne, Australia, in 2005 and continues to make jewelry as a passionate hobby. Her favorite materials include sterling silver, fine silver, precious and semiprecious stones, fabric, plastic and titanium. Mariann creates simple, modern, and balanced jewelry with occasional nods to the organic form. Find out more about Mariann at www.mariannmonika.blogspot.com and see her work at www.etsy.com/shop/mariannmonika.

Ann L. Lumsden is a goldsmith, designer, and Ottawa native. She strives to create pieces that are contemporary and classic. Through ongoing explorations of materials and techniques, both traditional and avant-garde, her work continues to evolve. She is a member of the Metal Arts Guild of Canada, and her pieces have twice been named Best in Show in their annual juried exhibitions.

Sim Luttin is a contemporary jeweler from Melbourne, Australia. She earned a BFA from the Royal Melbourne Institute of Technology and an MFA from Indiana University in metalsmithing and jewelry design. Sim exhibits in Australia, Europe, Asia, and the United States, and is represented by Charon Kransen, USA. Visit www.simluttin.com.

Kenneth C. MacBain is currently an Associate Professor and Coordinator of the Design and Crafts specialization at New Jersey City University. Most of his current work focuses on avant-garde body adornment and issues related to preciousness and social status. His work has been shown extensively and has been published in 19 books, as well as numerous periodicals.

Danielle Miller-Gilliam discovered her passion for metal in 1987 while at a high school summer art program and has been maintaining her jewelry studio since 1995. Danielle's work is known for its geometry and kinetic elements; subtle movements of gems, pearls, and metals generated by the wearer's body movements. Her work is shown at galleries throughout the United States and can be viewed at www.daniellemillerjewelry.com.

Rebeca Mojica is an award-winning chainmaille artist and instructor. She knows more than 100 weaves and is the founder of Blue Buddha Boutique, one of the largest chainmaille suppliers in the world. See her creations at www.bluebuddhaboutique.com.

Stephanie Morton lives and works in Toronto, Canada. Her work is a combination of formal training and her own experimentation. Her son is a constant source of feedback and ideas, but has refused to give up anymore of his plastic bugs for her to cast. Stephanie's work may be seen at www.madpashdesigns.com.

Andrea Pineros is a jewelry designer that has participated in workshops for the likes of Lanvin and Yves Saint Laurent in Paris. She is currently teaching at the renowned Paris jewelry school, AFEDAP. Andrea's personal work is comprised of unique pieces and small series pieces that she creates in her studio. Sensitive to the expressions of everyday life, Andrea gets inspiration from the fragility and strength of nature, the inheritance and transmission of a legacy, and the precious side of human beings. She creates meaningful and intimate objects that defy the world of mass production. You can discover her work in the website: http://designio.free.fr.

Karen Rakoski is a jewelry designer that experiments with wire and other leftover home improvement materials in upstate New York following a career in engineering and business. At her home, there is an abundance of wildlife and plants, so it is no surprise that the animals and flowers find their way into her writing, teaching, jewelry making, and, sometimes, into her house. Contact Karen at knrak@rochester.rr.com.

Davina Romansky is a metals artist with an aesthetic understanding of form and expression. She gives artistic identity to each work by combining conceptual and aesthetic beauty with technical proficiency. Davina has a BFA in metals from Rochester Institute of Technology and holds numerous design awards. Along with several other publications across the world, Davina has been published in the two previous Lark Crafts series books, *30 Minute Earrings* (2010) and *30 Minute Necklaces* (2010). Find out more about Davina's work at www.davinaromansky.com.

Brenda Schweder is the author *Junk to Jewelry* and *Vintage Redux*. A frequent BeadStyle contributor, Brenda has been published in all of Kalmbach Publishing's jewelry titles, as well as a number of pamphlets. Her newest book of fabulous projects is called *Steel Wire Jewelry* (Lark Crafts, 2011). Brenda is a Crystallized Swarovski Elements Ambassador. Visit her at www.brendaschweder.com or www.brendaschweder.blogspot.com.

Deb Soromenho is a seasoned traveler who loves to explore unique arts and cultures, and channels that passion into her metal jewelry. She named her studio A.W.E. Handcrafted Jewelry for her love of all things artsy, worldly, and earthy. Deb lives in Bethesda, MD, with her husband, son, and crazy cat.

Jennifer Surine has a BFA in metalsmithing and jewelry making from Grand Valley State University. She resides in Michigan, where she spends most of her time working in her studio creating and designing jewelry and sculptural work. For more information, visit www.bendthefish.com.

George Swanke's work highlights the imperfections that make things beautiful. His pieces are a manifestation of organic elegance, raw and refined; precious and worthless. He views life as a beautiful race in which he is just trying to keep up. Find George at www.georgeswanke.com.

Victoria Takahashi is a Washington native that loves to create and surround herself with objects and people that inspire her. She cannot begin to imagine a life without this wonderful self-indulgent addiction.

Victoria Tillotson is a jewelry designer and instructor of jewelry making at the School of Visual Arts in New York City. She is also the author of *Chic Metal: Modern Metal Jewelry to Make at Home*. Victoria's jewelry has been featured in numerous magazines such as *Lucky, Allure*, and *Essence*, as well as on television networks like MTV, Oxygen, and HSN. See more of her work at www.victoriatillotson.com.

John Tzelepis received his undergraduate degree from Skidmore College and his MFA in metals from Arizona State University. He has made jewelry and sculpture for over a decade. He exhibits work nationally and has been featured in several publications. See his work at www.johntzelepis.com.

Ingeborg Vandamme is a jewelry designer that works and lives in Amsterdam where she studied at the Gerrit Rietveld Academy. She experiments with different kinds of materials, such as combinations of paper, textiles, and metal. Ingeborg's jewelry is featured in numerous Lark Crafts publications, including several 500 series books, *The Art of Jewelry: Paper Jewelry* (2006), *The Art of Jewelry: Wood* (2008), *Stitched Jewelry* (2009), *30-Minute Earrings* (2010), and *30-Minute Necklaces* (2010). Find more of her work at www.ingeborgvandamme.nl.

Dace Vitola is a student at the Latvian Academy of Arts master's program in the Department of Metal Design. She is a designer who creates different kinds of objects in metal as unique jewelry art works.

Sara Westermark is a self-taught metalsmith who lives in Wilmington, NC. In her art, Sara celebrates life in its chaos, juxtaposed with the eternal struggle for order. She continues to be inspired by modern forms, human imperfection, and her Southern Coastal landscape. You can find her work at www.sarawestermark.com and www.etsy.com/shop/sarawestermark.

Maria Whetman combines traditional jewelry techniques and materials with non-traditional materials, making wearable artwork that brings a smile, tells a story, or creates a point of interest for the wearer. Her designs often incorporate reclaimed, printed steel packaging that she transforms into miniature compositions made of text, color, and pattern, making it unrecognizable from its original form. Find Maria's work at www.fluxplay.co.uk.

Cynthia B. Wuller is an artist, jewelry designer, and the author of *Inspired Wire*. Find her work in various Lark Crafts publications including *The Art of Jewelry: Paper Jewelry* (2006), *The Art of Jewelry: Wood* (2008), *Beading with Pearls* (2008), and *Pretty Little Presents* (2009).

Carole Zakkour grew up in Beirut, Lebanon, and moved to the United States, where she got a master's degree in horticulture. She loves to travel and is inspired by science, nature, and various cultures. Carole lives in Venice, CA, and can be reached at carolezakkour@msn.com.

Roberto Zanon is an architect and teaches at the Universities of Florence, Padua, and Venice and at the Academy of Fine Art of Torino. He has been a visiting professor at several universities throughout Europe and Asia, and he writes for numerous international magazines on the subjects of exhibition and product design. Roberto owns a studio in Italy and can be found at www.robertozanon.it.